Praise for
MEANING IS THE MISSION

"Understand the essence of entrepreneurship with this transformative book. It's more than a guide—it's a roadmap for conquering the inner battles every leader faces."

—TIM KEININGHAM, *New York Times* bestselling
author of *The Wallet Allocation Rule,* and the J. Donald
Kennedy Endowed Chair at St. John's University

"This book is a practical and inspiring guidebook on unleashing your inner purpose and harnessing your God-given talents by connecting purpose in your work. It's a must read for any founder or CEO!"

—DAVE DYER, CEO and Partner, Manifesto

"Mike Kelly challenges leaders to see the gap between the organization they want and the organization they have. Anyone who wants better results and less excuses will benefit! Read this book!"

—JAMES MCBRIDE, CEO, Lion's Share FCU

"In *Meaning is the Mission,* Mike Kelly provides the language and insights that make it possible for the rest of us to discover our own truth, avoid disappointment, and to accelerate the arrival of our own success in the service of others."

—**MIKE MERCER**, CEO and Founder, COOPR8 Consulting

"Work without meaning is empty. Mike cuts right to the core of the issue with one simple question: Is the way you work working?"

—**RAY LANCASTER**, CEO, Pyramid FCU

"Experiencing Mike Kelly is like grabbing a lightning bolt of enthusiastic joy! It's thrilling to be inspired to live freely out of a heart of love and service to others by a Great Communicator."

—**DANGEROUS DAVE RUTH**, ThD

MEANING
IS
THE
MISSION

UNDERSTANDING THE SYMPTOMS

OF SUCCESS **AND HOW TO**

GET DREAMS DONE ON PURPOSE

MIKE KELLY

WINDERMERE
PRESS

COPYRIGHT © 2024 MIKE KELLY
All rights reserved.

MEANING IS THE MISSION
Understanding the Symptoms of Success and
How to Get Dreams Done on Purpose
First Edition

ISBN   978-1-962341-01-1   *Hardcover*
         978-1-962341-00-4   *Paperback*
         978-1-962341-02-8   *Ebook*

I dedicate this book to my wife, Jessica. Fav, I love you more than words alone can express, I'm so thankful to you that you always see my symptoms of success before I do, and I'm grateful to God that He decided to make us one.

CONTENTS

"THERE IS NO FEAR IN LOVE; COMPLETE LOVE DRIVES OUT
FEAR. FEAR HAS TO DO WITH PUNISHMENT, AND ANYONE WHO
IS AFRAID HAS NOT BEEN COMPLETED IN LOVE."

1 JOHN 4: 18

MEANING IS THE MISSION

Isn't it strange that we're spending more money than ever to make work better—only to see it get worse?

Billions and billions of dollars and hours, and for what? Poor employee satisfaction scores, terrible customer satisfaction scores, and the worse news of all: many industries, including the one I'm currently serving, are collapsing.

Why?

Answering this question is the reason I'm writing this book.

In this book, I'm going to lay out the argument that we are working harder than ever to solve symptoms rather than root cause, which is why all this effort is going to waste. Simply put, we aren't working on the right things!

Finding the root cause solution is the puzzle I help my clients put together each day, and it's the puzzle I'll put together for you in this book.

Here's how we get started solving the root cause problem: first, we make sure we're asking the right questions. In other words, we must make sure we have all the puzzle pieces out of the box if we want to solve it!

Like: Is the way you work *working?* You, the human: are you working as designed? In your work life, how is it going for you? Only by answering this question for ourselves can we discover how it's going for the group of humans we work with, and ask, "How are we working? Is it *working?* How do we know?"

Are we spending all sorts of time and effort on symptoms, such as: *Where are we working—in the office or remotely? Is AI going to steal all our jobs? Do you have a fixed or growth mindset?*

If those are the main questions we're asking, then we're

working very hard to become nothing more than a poor man's robot. We are too obsessed with technical skills and ignoring power skills. When was the last time you saw wisdom on a resume? (I never have!)

A better question to ask is this: did a subtle lie slip into our bloodstream, and now imposter syndrome is the pervasive problem in our worklife? When did the joy of learning something new get replaced with the fear of being found out as a fraud?

Imposter syndrome shows up in three big forms:

1. The Perfectionist Imposter that is never satisfied with success, even when wildly exceeding it.

2. The Poser Imposter that avoids measuring success.

3. The Ponzi Imposter who is the psychopath fixated on themselves, above all, at the expense of all, no matter what cost.

This subtle lie has turned into a river of fear flooding companies where most people are running scared without even a basic understanding of who they are, the jobs they do, or how their unique gifting works—ignoring gaps or what to do next.

In this book, you'll learn why these things have compounded to create a massive blind spot that is keeping the root cause solution hidden from view, and so many people stuck in an Imposter Prison of Fear.

I want to bring awareness to this issue, get you involved in the escape plan, and then help you implement it so you can support your success from now on!

But, how do you know if you're in Imposter Prison, trapped by fear at best, and at worst, something invisible?

How do you escape this prison and find freedom to be who God made you to be, working on things that matter alongside people you trust?

How do you use a simple system to support your success to overcome the challenges of working on willpower alone?

Lastly, how do you get dreams done on purpose?

These are the questions I want to ask and answer together in this book because these questions and answers are the path to root cause problem and solution—yet not discussed often enough, or at all, especially at work.

THE MISSION OF THIS BOOK

My mission in this book is to get you to consider the questions that matter most to you. At work there's one big question we are ignoring and it's the root cause solution hiding in plain sight.

What's the meaning in the mission?

Why do you care? Why does it matter to you? If you don't ask the question, the answer stays hidden.

The meaning in your mission has to matter to you in some way that will move you forward no matter what, and that meaning must connect in some way to your company's mission or the company won't succeed.

This book is for the eighty percent of people who want something different and are willing to do the work to make things better. Unless and until each person on the team has the power to go hunt for the meaning in their own mission and attach that to the work in front of them, which then is a known building block into the bigger story being told at the company, it's not going to work.

The meaning can be anything but complete self-interest. This is not another book on the search for meaning in your life, there are plenty of those already. Instead, this book is an invitation to escape this prison of fear and become who God made you to be: a human being at work, working as designed.

You are employed by your company, your company is designed to generate profit, and it's your job to quantify how you help create that end.

Every great relationship is an equal exchange of value, including the relationship you have with your work life.

What value are you contributing first? Do you understand deeply so you can evaluate your progress to goal while also working on what's next?

Only you can stop you, and you won't start if you won't stare down the lies you've been telling yourself.

This is a lifestyle call I'm making to you, not a diet change. This is an opportunity to completely rebuild your heart-set to feed your mindset to give you energy to build new skillsets.

This is your chance right now to stop working so hard to lie to yourself, and instead, relax in the realization that living in a prison of fear isn't the answer—and that you can work hard to add facts to these feelings of being an imposter in order to breakthrough in your worklife.

Do this work I'm offering you for six months and deal with the consequences of building on the truth of moving towards being who God made you to be. As you move, the system is designed to make you consider what's working and what's not, and you'll make adjustments on your path that work for you. This will be a great victory!

Meaning is the fuel for your mission. It's what makes

it inevitable. If you are locked in on the meaning of your mission, you won't be stopped because you can't be stopped. Even in the most difficult part of the struggle—and struggle you will—if you have meaning in your heart, mind, body, spirit, it will give you strength to keep moving forward.

If each employee's mission doesn't have a chance to be fulfilled, the company's mission has zero chance to be fulfilled, either. In fact, the questions I ask CEOs about how to run their companies effectively are not all that different from the questions employees must ask themselves about their own work lives.

I ask CEOs three big questions:

1. Is the way your company works working? How do you know?

2. Is everyone working on what matters most? How do you measure it?

3. How do you also work on what's next? How do you make tomorrow, today?

If those are the questions CEOs must answer, then here are the three big questions each employee must answer, too:

1. Is the way I work working?

2. Am I working only on what matters most?

3. How do I also work on what's next?

I want to focus my effort in these pages to combine these two ideas. I want you to imagine these ideas as Lego building blocks that must snap together to build whatever it is you a building. These ideas connect; you have to make them "snap" together, or you will not be working in alignment with the goals for the company or for the meaning in your mission, and you definitely won't understand your symptoms of success—never mind being intentional about getting your dreams done on purpose.

What CEOs want and what employees want can converge to create alignment a grassroots level, not just top-down.

By creating this understanding first, then we are creating common ground to build upon together.

THINK AND FEEL WITH HEARTSET, FIRST

Each one of us has a deeper mode of knowing—what I'm calling "Heartset", something we're going deep on together in this book.

Heartset is where your deepest thinking and feeling is done and where language can't quite capture what it is you know to be true—and yet you still know!

Understanding your heartset is the breakthrough you'll earn from reading this book and it's what I want you to consider as we begin this journey. We are going to talk about these things and more so you can break your blind spot wide open, understand what you care about and why you care, and make the mission matter more than ever.

Mindset alone can't solve your problem; it's not the root cause solution, and you have way more ability on hand to tap into than just mindset alone. Have you ever heard anyone admit to having a fixed mindset? Of course not, at least when there's more than one person in the conference room. You'll get the scarlet letter of "Loser!" if you admit this at work, so of course no one says it out loud—too much risk to paycheck and career path.

You will be tempted to jump to the punchline and skip the work it takes to create your path to success. That will be up to you, but ask yourself:

Right now, is *the way you work* working?

If yes, good for you—perhaps you'll give this book to someone else who can make use of its message.

If not, then read on.

But before you jump in, I want to challenge you with this idea:

Willpower alone is for amateurs.

You need a simple system to support your success. You

have to break blind spots, do the goals that go with your role, and use a simple system to support your success. The world is complex and moving faster than ever. You may have *symptoms* of success, and now you must learn how to create your standard of success, invest in it, manage it, and make your mission matter! That's root cause solution!

Heartset feeds mindset so you can build new skillsets to understand the meaning in your mission and support your success in a simple system.

That's where we are going in this book together.

Are you ready? Of course you aren't—I'm about to rock your world. But come with me anyway, because you need to know that you do, in fact, have what it takes!

Let's go!

PART ONE

MEANING IS THE MISSION

"My heart is in anguish within me; the terrors of death have fallen upon me."

Psalm 55:4

CHAPTER ONE

IMPOSTER PRISON

In thirteen years, I went from the copy room to the corner office of a $300M company. I was thirty-eight years old.

In my four years as CEO of our 1,700 person team, our company achieved incredible success by any measure available, and our team had transformed our company into being one of the leading growth businesses in the financial technology sector.

Our company was valued at $925M, our net income was up 119%, our profitability grew 79%, we added 300 customers and retained an all-time high of existing clients, our free cash went from zero to $45M: all outstanding metrics of success.

Our team made more money than ever, and I did, too. I reached my highest earning year up until that point in my career, and was thrilled to learn that my contract was going to be renewed for another five years.

The dream had become reality, our measures of success proved it, and we were on top of the world, in great position for more.

And then?

I got fired.

"Ousted", as the newspaper headlines read.

Why?

I got fired because I was motivated by fear. I was motivated by fear because I didn't know how or why to understand how to be a whole human being working in service to others.

I got fired because my lack of mature understanding had me guessing at the root cause problems instead of knowing how to evaluate the truth.

I got fired because I didn't understand what mattered

most.

I got fired because I didn't understand my symptoms of success. Because I was working on willpower alone instead of using a simple system to support my success.

I got fired because I was fighting the ghosts of my past—I wasn't recognizing the situation for what it was, instead recognizing it for what I wanted it to be.

The details of that story are mine, but I'm not alone in them. In fact, the things that got me fired are the same issues that plague many of you reading this book and seeking deeper understanding.

So why is work such a struggle?

I believe it's a struggle because we aren't understanding that we are solving symptoms and not root cause.

It's a struggle because so many people are in Imposter Prison and trapped by fear but can't, or won't, recognize it for what it actually is: a lie!

It's a lie that has become true for you. It's the root cause solution that's hiding in your blind spot. And it's where we start.

THE LIE THAT HAS BECOME TRUE

The thing about lies is that you don't always see them as such. In fact, they're often quite believable. A great lie has enough truth in it so that you'll consider it, and ultimately be captured by its promise. It can't be based on too much actual evidence, though, or you'd understand it as a lie.

Imposter Syndrome is a popular topic at work these days. You hear all the time; people cop to it frequently and casually and as no big deal.

"I totally have imposter syndrome. I feel like a total fraud all the time."

It's almost a virtue signal at this point, something to be admired, meant to get people thinking, "Look at how vulnerable and comfortable he is admitting it!" All great lies are subtle and sneaky because they are built on a small slice of the truth—that's how they pass your sniff test.

There are three types of imposters, I've learned:

1. The **Perfectionist Imposter** knows that even great isn't good enough—only perfection will do—and therefore success is unattainable.

2. The **Poser Imposter** sounds amazing but avoids actual accountability so that success can never be measured—way more talk than walk.

3. The **Ponzi Imposter** is a psychopath who preys on imposters and posers to get what they want no matter the consequences.

It's too much to handle, I know, because it's too close to home for each one of us—I'm right there with you! It's terrible when you put words to all this because from now forward, it'll be in your heart, asking you, "Are you being a poser, or are you being who God made you to be?"

I did a keynote talk in the spring of 2023 to 1,400 executives on this very topic. Afterward, a member of the audience, a guy in his mid-thirties, found his way to me. He grabbed me by the shoulders and told me plainly:

"I loved your talk, and I hated your talk, too!"

The big smile on his face told me I wasn't in harm's way. It's so rare that people will tell you to your face what they don't like, so I was thrilled by this moment.

"Perfect!", I said, smiling a smile to match his and grabbing his shoulders, too, so now we were embracing one another. "Tell me, shoot it straight!"

"It's like you were reading my mail when you were talking about imposter syndrome. I have a new job—well, it's actually been eighteen months, so I guess it's not that new—but imposter syndrome has a hold of me bad and it was about to break me. And now you ruined it for me!"

"Ruined it?" I said, mirroring his question.

"Yes, you totally ruined it! I'm sitting there listening to you, and I'm thinking, *This freaking guy just took my last excuse away. Why am I struggling like this—so fearful, such a perfectionist? Why am I not enjoying this learning process and focusing on becoming better at what I do?*

He made my eyes well up with tears, this guy. I was so happy for him, and for me, too.

This prison of fear is not the place we are designed to live. He recognized it, and was ready to take action himself to bust out of the prison.

What a win!

ARE YOU A PERFECTIONIST, POSER, OR PONZI?

Imposter syndrome usually rears its ugly head when you are doing something new or thinking about doing something new.

The voice in your head says, "Oh, come on man, you can't do that! You have a lot of nerve even thinking that!"

The voice in your head is mean because it is a liar.

The reality is that when you are doing something new, you are the bottom of a brand new, very steep learning curve—you are correct to recognize that you don't know everything you need to know yet because that's true!

And it's why you went for this new job, in order to learn something new!

If you didn't think you could do it, why did you go to it? It's because deep down, in the places in your heart where you do your deepest thinking but language isn't available, the truth is struggling to get out.

When I became CEO, I was constantly panicked for the first eighteen months. It was the very bottom of a massive new learning curve with high risk and reward—and everyone was watching (or so I thought!).

I was measuring my self-worth based on my performance. Caring about your performance is good, but building your self-worth on your performance alone is bad.

The truth in any new role or endeavor is simple: you are learning something new! It might turn out that you can't do this new thing in front of you, but you literally can't know that at the beginning because you haven't done it yet.

The lie you tell yourself in reaction to the discomfort of the novel is that, eventually, inevitably, you will be found out as a fraud, a phony, all talk and no walk. Deeper still is the more devasting lie that has become true for you: that you are worthless.

Worth. Less.

That you are not worthy, that you don't matter, and that of course it's because of who you are that you don't have what it takes.

Lies, lies, and more lies.

The truth is the human beings are made by design to learn, grow, and expand.

Look no further than you as a child. You are made for

this; it's how you work.

You don't even need to go back that far to gather the evidence that you are built to learn, grow, and expand.

I didn't know then what I know now, but I was an imposter among imposters. People who were creating massive results at their companies, the top ten percent of all performers, were here and all were lacking something that was unidentifiable.

We were all searching for self-worth through performance, and it became clear that the bigger the results, the more devastating the drop in self-worth—because the results were surely the answer to filling the black hole in my soul. So, you hustle and achieve and are powered by fear. You go do something amazing and the pop of satisfaction is real but brief. Coming down off the high is a doozy.

And more, the high is shorter on each hit.

I hear CEOs say, "our culture is empowered!", yet all decisions consolidate to the top of the pyramid because that's where the power consolidates.

The paradox of companies is that they are built to converge all "important" things to do the top of the pyramid while most of the humans are the bottom of the pyramid, and all humans are designed naturally to learn, expand, and grow—but are contained in this constricted environment.

The structure of companies blocks the humans working inside the company from creating results in a mode of operation that is more natural in its design.

Don't get me wrong; I am not for chaos mode. I'm all for infrastructure that creates more clarity. After all, success means helping each person on the team to only do work that matters to the company's bottom line.

Read this sentence clearly, CEOs: I know this is your best path to profitability because I've done it.

Here's the real deal:

1. Your top ten percent of performers are going to perform no matter what you do— that's how you get to be in the top ten percent of all performers.

2. Your bottom ten percent of performers are not going to perform for reasons that are hidden to you—and they probably won't or they would have done so already.

3. The other eighty percent of your workforce are desperate for something different. If you only help to remove barriers for twenty percent of this group, your company will fly sky high.

Your top performers are you—probably suffering from imposter syndrome perfectionists all seeking self-worth through performance. You hustled to get here, so why can't the rest of these people, right?

Wrong! You are uniquely damaged and trying to fill the black hole in your heart with something that makes the black hole's gravitational force pull more into its field of destruction.

Your next group will have a mix of perfectionists with a proper dose of poser. Success is just out of sight for this group because they find new and clever ways to avoid the accountability to get the yes or no answer to the question in each person's heart: "Do I have what it takes?"

Top performers like getting the answer: *Yes, I have what it takes but I should have done more* or *No, I don't have what it takes because of course I was right the whole time about being a fraud!*

But that's not you thinking. That's the lie doing your thinking for you.

THE PERFECTIONIST IMPOSTER

There are people who are never happy with what they've accomplished, even when they've surpassed their goal. Top performers at work are the most obvious example of this.

Typically, this group of "A Players" are performance-driven, approval-seeking, hard-charging, win-at-all-costs kind of people. Many CEOs are in this group.

What has also become clear in the many interactions I've had with those in this group is that perfectionism arises from shame.

Shame not that you *did something wrong*, but that *you*

are wrong, and this belief powers the work effort to accomplish results no matter what's in the way. You know this person if you aren't that person—they just get stuff done and there's an edge, perhaps an anger that's underneath—a seething, it seems, and it fuels the fire each day.

Something happens early on in your life to convince you of this and you start defending yourself against it. Slowly, bit by bit, you build a force field around yourself, a barrier through which no one can see what you know deep down is actually true: that you suck, that you are a fraud, that you are a big fat liar, and that you secretly disdain people that can't see your true nature because it's so obvious.

If these words resonate, then you might be a perfectionist imposter.

For you, it's all about gaining approval for your life through performance. What better place to do that than in corporate America? The corporate model rewards performance and the results you create are what matters most. *How* you create them? Not as important—and often, not important at all!

You got a new job or are working on a new project, and you think, deep down in places where words don't capture what you're actually feeling:

"Oh shit, here we go again—I can't do this, I know I can't do this, and how soon is my boss going to figure it out?"

But if you're a real perfectionist, you quickly snap out of it and keep moving forward:

"Screw it, I might as well go down in flames then!"

Some of that isn't a terrible thing, of course, and I imagine it's actually a good indicator that you're an actual human being and not a robot.

But too much of it, and you lose your way.

For a person suffering from perfectionist imposter syndrome, there is rarely a more painful thing than receiving a compliment.

At the peak of my perfectionism, there was nothing more painful than to hear someone say nice things about me. It was like a knife in my side and shamed me secretly because I would think "Ugh, are you this much of an idiot to not see what is so obviously true? I'm a total fraud and I have no idea what I'm doing!"

That was if I received the compliment from someone that I didn't really idolize.

If the compliment was from someone that I looked up to or was a role model in some fashion, then the compliment would send me to cloud nine!

"Malcolm Gladwell just told me I gave a great speech!"

Oh, there was no greater drug for me than something like this (which actually happened, by the way!). I would get so high from that and it would be the air in my lungs for days and sometimes weeks. It would boost my feelings of self-worth in a way that was incredibly powerful, but ultimately temporary and shallow.

Malcolm Gladwell didn't know me. I met him for fifteen minutes prior to our client conference (he's super nice, extremely interesting and didn't disappoint on any of the vectors you might imagine if you know who he is).

I didn't know how to take his compliment because my understanding of my performance was built on a lie.

THE POSER IMPOSTER

For the poser imposter, it's nearly the opposite dilemma. The poser hates measuring success because he is convinced he doesn't have what it takes to succeed, either, and doesn't want the judgement—it's too much!

The Poser Imposter sounds amazing but never does anything actually amazing, or often enough to justify the talk.

It's a "walk the talk" issue with the poser: lots of talk, not enough walk.

The poser avoids adding up success with as much energy as the perfectionist avoids being satisfied by success—it's a parody of how God designed us, and gets worse the more you work to ignore it.

Once you are aware of it, though, it's momentarily worse because now, you can't not know what I'm telling you is true for you!

And me, and each of us.

You don't need to stay an imposter, either a perfectionist or a poser, although you might always get those feelings now and again—with work and understanding, though, you'll start to feel the joy of knowing what's happening and the ability to connect your heartset to your mindset and say "Aha! I know this!", and move your way through as a student and teacher, not an imposter parody.

THE PONZI IMPOSTER

Ponzis are the smallest segment of imposters, because Ponzis are psychopaths, and psychopaths are only about four percent of the total population of people. There are thankfully not that many of them out there.

But run into a Ponzi Imposter at work, especially the very clever ones and when you are held prisoner as a perfectionist or a poser, and the Ponzi will take you out with bias and with no holds barred, either.

The Ponzi imposter has none of the problems of the perfectionist or the poser because they are less than human. The Ponzi does not have guilt or shame or joy and happiness or insecurity. Instead, the Ponzi is only focused on one thing: getting what they want when it's wanted no matter what.

At work, Ponzis like middle management because it's easier to hide in plain sight and they can more easily prey on the perfectionists and the posers. There's not too much of a spotlight on them, or at least for very long, and what's valued there anyway is getting results. The Ponzi knows how to prey on the striving of the perfectionist and the fear of judgement of the poser in order to get what they want.

If you've ever worked for a Ponzi, you know what I'm talking about.

If this makes no sense to you, you might be a Ponzi!

I worked for a Ponzi, and he not only fired me, but he also aimed to destroy me with character assassination. I can see the signals now, but then? I fell for it hook, line, and sinker.

I met him while interviewing for the CEO job I've been discussing. He was on the Board and a super nice guy, well-liked by his peers. He was a social butterfly and harmless enough, or so I thought.

With what I know now, he was no perfectionist all talk, no walk. His team told me exactly what I needed to know right before I was going into a meeting with him one on one.

"Mike, do you think he's ready for this meeting with you?"

They were all chuckling; this was his inner circle of direct reports.

"Of course!" I responded earnestly, thinking, *That's a weird question, why wouldn't he be?*

I didn't think much of it, and we had a beautiful meeting.

All the right things were said and I left on cloud nine. After that, though? Hardly anything we talked about was what we worked on, and much of what we discussed this psycho said we never did.

One of the great indicators of working with a Ponzi is when you find yourself questioning everything you do to an intense level in a manner that you don't do with almost anyone else.

I think the kids now call this gaslighting, but in plain spoken language, the Ponzi has an elite ability to make you believe it's *you*, and not them, to keep you chasing the things you talked about but aren't actually important at all to the Ponzi.

The first time I met this guy was on the interview process and he kept asking me the same question over and over:

1. "Kelly, do you have a backbone?"

2. "Kelly, have you ever made a hard decision?"

3. "Kelly, have you ever fired anyone?"

4. "Kelly, how am I supposed to believe you have a spine?"

He said it twelve times if he said it once—even to the point where I thought, *Wow, this guy is really worried about this!*

It turns out this guy has no bones in his body, never mind a backbone! Weak character, no integrity, can't make a clear decision to save his life—ugh, he's the worst kind of leader.

But I wasn't mature enough to understand what was happening, never mind evaluate the situation for what it was instead of what I was imagining it to be, and he played me to the very end and won a battle that I didn't know was being fought (and neither did I recognize that my battle wasn't with him!). I was insecure, trapped in a prison of fear, in search of perfection—a perfect mark for a Ponzi!

I eventually sat down with him one-on-one to get clear on our working relationship. It wasn't working for me or our team; he was disruptive, and now in a position to let that disruption ripple throughout our organization.

He was three months into his Chairmanship and it was a disaster, so I just asked him straight up:

"How do you think this is going for us? Do you think you want to continue?"

Wrong question, and a lie to my face as an answer.

"You're right, I need to focus more and support you and the team," and a bunch of other right-sounding cliches.

Two weeks after the compensation chair informed me that my contract was getting renewed for another five years along with a handsome raise, I got fired.

By the Ponzi.

"Ok, I understand you want to go another way, but help me understand why I'm getting fired?"

"It's just time, it's just what we want to do—we're gonna go in another direction. Why don't you go talk to your wife and let us know if you want to step down or be fired? It's up to you. We'll give you 24 hours to let us know."

We had signed a contract when I began my employment, and in it was this circumstance in particular—termination was already agreed upon, and I knew the terms.

Twenty minutes after the meeting ended, my phone starts blowing up with messages from the team and soon after that, with messages from the industry journals and websites regarding what happened.

Twenty-four hours? A lie, one of many.

But that's how Ponzis roll and that is an example of the last gasp of a Ponzi. The Ponzi will attack you, smear you, try to damage your character because there is no other choice, it's their only way to survive.

I saw this same guy at an industry conference many years later. I had forgiven him and more importantly myself by this time, and felt moved to say hello and apologize for my part in a poor ending.

It was an important step for me and helped me also understand he hadn't changed at all—without missing a beat, he spoke to me as if nothing had happened—he was totally relaxed. It shocked me, actually, and made me realize that he hadn't thought about me since that last meeting and he wasn't going to think about me the moment I left this momentary meet up.

The gifts of God are many and this was one of them—it matured me in ways that otherwise, I don't know how I would have learned these lessons.

Now, I can spot Imposters a mile away, and can serve Perfectionists and Posers and help them, if they have ears to hear, to understand they are trapped in a prison of fear, just like I was. And the Ponzis? The minute I decide, "Ah, this is person is a Ponzi", I know to take action, swift and sure.

If you let a Ponzi hang around, or if you hang around them, they'll damage you. It's what they do.

THE LIE OF THE IMPOSTER

So, what is the lie that your imposter is telling you?

Is the lie that you can't do your job? If you got a new job, this might actually be true! Which is why you wanted to the new job in the first place, because you get to learn something new.

But not being able to do the job—you can't know if that's true or not because you haven't *done* the job. This is the subtle truth that you are wise to understand!

But, deep down, you believe it's true and that it's obvious not just to you, but to everyone that comes in contact with you.

So you just start saying it out loud to name and claim the little bit of truth that's not very dangerous at all in order to keep any further inspection at bay. It keeps everyone at a distance, and at the same time, you gain credit for being very self-aware!

"Yup, I'm a total imposter, I have no idea how to do this job." This is the lazy way to admit something to the world that you believe is true—that you're a fraud and don't belong—but isn't actually the deepest thing you are worried about.

The worst part of imposter syndrome is that you keep the deeper truth of it secret. You might admit a piece of it, and you might be working hard to ignore all of it, but the secret puts you into isolation because ultimately, it feels deeply embarrassing. Instead of the joy of learning something new—like being a new CEO—you are cratered by the fear of being exposed for not knowing how to do it.

Isolation is where lies can grow big. They gain power. The stories you tell yourself in your head are devasting and frequent, and your inner critic is vicious.

These subtle lies set you adrift. They isolate you. They embarrass you; they shame you.

The subtlety of the lie has helped you drift toward becoming sub-human, just like I did. You compartmentalize your life so that you can pretend to ignore the things that truly matter, like being loved by God so that you can love those you love the most.

Imposter syndrome had isolated me and I didn't know it. I was hiding behind an aura of strength and wellness, energy for everything, with very little that wasn't interesting or worthy of addressing. I have a lot of natural energy and enough of it to run hard for long stretches of time, and when I was CEO of a bigger company, I learned to hide in plain sight.

When I was first a CEO, I'd often hear, "Wow, you are so young, with young kids, and this is a big job—how do you do it all?"

Good question. I'd answer, "Fear. I'm afraid to fail."

And we'd laugh together! What I was saying was true but there was never any further inspection on the obvious point I was making—that nothing good gets built on fear alone, and nothing good is sustained on fear alone. Fear is built on a lie. It's fake.

I didn't understand the paradox of it all at all.

Here's the thing about imposter syndrome: you end up doing little subtle things that make it come true. They are almost imperceptible to anyone but you, but these tiny little decisions end up sabotaging your growth because deep down you know it can't true—that you are made for something more.

You do little things to shame yourself, you take little tiny pieces of your soul and remove them each day. You put them into their own compartments, locked away so that you don't have to look at them.

Imposter syndrome is subtle so that it can set in. Once it sets in, it starts to shame you. It shames you so you'll keep it secret. It stays a secret so that it isolates you. It isolates you so you'll dehumanize yourself inch by inch until the job is complete.

You believe the lie is true for you.

The lie of imposter syndrome had set in early in my life and had grown in such strength that it actually enabled me to become very successful in the way we define success at work —which is based on results.

Few people break free of it. Most are held prisoner by it.

To break free of it, you first have to see it. But this can be hard to do because:

1. Imposter syndrome has you convinced you are the problem, and

2. Imposter has compartmentalized you enough so that you'll shred everyone else to make yourself feel good (but not too good)

This is your best indicator of the depth of the lie that you made true for you.

One of the best ways to spot this lie is to look in a mirror. You have hundreds of mirrors available to you each day, and if you really pay attention, they will tell you *so* much. They'll help you connect your heartset to your mindset so you can build your skillsets.

CHAPTER TWO

YOUR BLIND SPOT MIRRORS

Performance is good. Building your self-worth on *only* your performance is bad.

It's a black hole in your heart. The better you perform, the shorter the feeling of satisfaction for performing well lasts. It's a drug, and you build more and more of a tolerance with each hit.

The truth is that if you are growing, expanding, and learning in your life and career, the symptoms of success will always be with you and remind you that you are going in the right direction.

Here's how it played out for me.

1. I had good dose of imposter syndrome as a first-time

CEO of a big company making a big step up in job responsibilities.

2. Deep down, I was worried I didn't have what it takes and knew for sure it was an issue about me as a person more than anything else.

3. I was worried I didn't have integrity; I just didn't know that was my blind spot yet.

4. When I met people that I perceived didn't have integrity, they made me wild—in particular when they were my bosses.

5. I worked for two Chairmen in my time as CEO, and the second one had zero integrity. He made me crazy. I wasn't yet mature enough to understand why, because the lie that I made true created a huge blind spot for me, and I couldn't see him for who he was or me for who I was.

6. I ran headlong into trouble there, and it's what got me fired.

Here's the thing I didn't know then but know very well now:

The things that bug me the most about other people are the things I believe are true for me, too.

Deep down, imposter syndrome had taken hold of me already. I believed the lie that I didn't have the ability to be a real CEO because I had a massive amount of insecurity, a total lack of integrity, and weak character.

Cars now have "blind spot indicators" in the side view mirrors and tech that will alert you that something is in your blind spot so you don't get into an accident.

Do you have that in your life and work?

No!

Not yet, anyway. You have to work overtime to get good at this part and here's why:

1. Your blind spot is blind to you. You can't see it!

2. In the case of imposter syndrome, it's hidden beneath

the rubble of a lie that turned true for you.

Here's an exercise to get you closer to a list of things that are your true blind spots:

1. Think about the person that drives you the craziest at work. Picture them in your mind's eye right now.

2. Think about the person that makes "your teeth itch", the person that sets you on edge who you can't stand.

We all have one (or more). I suspect your person popped into your mind immediately. Me too!

I love putting things on a one to ten scale because it gives you a simple, clean comparative framework to talk things through. (Just make sure you're clear on what constitutes a one and what constitutes a ten.) So imagine your mood on a scale of one to ten—one being the calmest flow state you can imagine, and ten being a frazzled, chaotic, anxious, frustrated mess.

The person you're thinking of? They *immediately* take you

to an eleven. No warmup. You see them and you're ready
to explode.

Why is that?

What about this person drives you insane?

Here's the big unlock, the nugget of information that
makes this whole book worth reading.

*The thing that bugs you the most about this person is the thing
you probably hate most about yourself.*

*And the thing you most hate about you is probably a lie that
you are worried is actually true.*

*So you bury it, ignore it, and push it out of the way into a tiny
compartment that stays hidden—or so you tell yourself.*

You can see your imposter in that person, in other words,
and it's easier for you to rage at them than to consider
this might be the thing you are most worried about being
true for you. It's too close to home for you and sits in that
deep part of your heart where you don't have language but

where truth lives.

When I was held prisoner by this, I was unable to connect the feeling to my thinking. Now that I understand, I still get that initial feeling of going to eleven on a ten scale—but now, I'm glad for it because I understand I'm seeing things correctly, I'm just not burdened by it because it may or may not be true of this person and it's not true of me.

This is what I mean by "heartset first"—it's your deepest thinking and deepest feeling that doesn't necessarily have language just yet. Is it wisdom percolating, perhaps? How dare you even consider it, right?

Of course you can consider it! You can get wisdom and get understanding if you understand heartset is the first of the tools you have at your disposal to be in this wonderful world.

HOW DOES THE WORLD SEE YOU?

There's a curious thing that happens when you compare

the compliments you receive from people in your world to the critic in your head.

They are almost never aligned.

The compliments you receive from everyone else are based on how you show up in the world—they represent how the world sees you.

The critic in your head is how you see yourself. When your critic's feedback is out of whack with the world's feedback, that's your opportunity to learn what's true and what's not.

Typically, it's hard for the perfectionist imposter to list any compliments about themselves at all: "Oof, I have a hard time receiving compliments!" Yet ask this same person for their critique of themselves and they'll say something like "Oh my, how much time do you have? We are going to need more time because the list is long!"

Isn't that curious? It is! Consider what's happening here because it will help you do a gap analysis on your own.

In my experience, it is, and it's what I want you to explore in this section and simply reflect on it so you can start to understand the picture for what is actually is instead of what you wished it was.

HOW DO YOU SEE YOU?

Set your phone timer for thirty minutes and take out a legal pad. Write out all the things you stink at, all the problems you bring to anything you attempt, all the gaps and the headaches you face on a regular basis.

Do it now and come back with your long list of things you aren't good at.

This is where imposter syndrome gets real. The list of things you aren't good at is long, according to you.

Why, when the request is to critique yourself, does it come *so* easily?

The reason this exercise is easy is that you are an imposter seeking perfection so that you can fill the black hole in

your heart with performance and results to prove your
worth.

If perfectionism isn't your problem, and instead posing
is the main issue—these results will flip—it's a paradox.
Your list of internal compliments will be way longer that
your criticisms, and your willingness to accept the criticisms of others will increase because it won't be so punish-
ing because the judgement is now in its proper place.

At work, it is about results—that's how you earn the cash
and prizes, including better work that challenges you to
improve!

What if this exercise was actually hard? What if you
couldn't easily come up with a list of things you do wrong?

Then you're an imposter avoiding accountability. The exercise is hard because you are working extra hard to ignore
your faults to the same end as your imposter colleagues—
in both cases, success is perverted and is either never
enough or never attained.

Here's where it gets tricky!

The list you made contains the things you know about. What about things that are hidden from you?

In corporate America, you might hear them as "blind spots", and since we'll be using an analogy of driving your vision as a vehicle, it's apt.

ADDING UP THE PIECES OF THE PUZZLE

Why was it so difficult to get out a list of things you are good at or compliments you receive, to the point where the compliments, at times, feel like daggers in your heart?

I think what happens here is that we work very hard to put these things into compartments and tuck them away and in this way, start to disassemble ourselves from the original manufacturers design.

The compliments can't possibly be true, so I'll dismiss them.

The critic in my head is certainly correct, but I'll keep that to myself because it's too embarrassing (or, I'll let just a little bit out so no one looks more closely than that, including me).

The big problem is when a subtle lie becomes true for you, it then becomes invisible. You don't see it because it is simply the truth that you live.

It's a distortion, and my aim with this book is to help you break free of it.

COMPLIMENTS EXERCISE

Now, on your legal pad, write down the list of compliments you most frequently receive. (If you can't write down at least three, you are lying to yourself—stop it.)

Once your list is set, I want you to set your phone timer again for thirty minutes, and ask yourself, "Why do I get these compliments?"

If you're anything like me, you might find yourself dismissing each compliment because it's praise for doing something that, for you, is as easy for you as breathing.

They might even feel painful to receive—almost like the work you're putting in on harder things is going unnoticed. "That? That's nothing for me—don't you see this other thing over there I'm putting in *real* effort on?"

Here's the exercise I want you to do:

1. Turn your phone timer on for sixty minutes this time.

2. Place these lists in front of you and read them out loud so you can hear yourself saying them.

3. What themes jump off the page at you?

4. What of these things is there actual evidence for, and what might be only your feelings? Feelings matter, they are a gift from God and not be ignored! But feelings alone are faulty guides, and you need to add some facts to your feelings.

5. Circle the things that you think might be lies. Just consider them. Can you prove them?

COMPARTMENTS ARE A COVERUP

It wasn't until about three years after I got fired from being CEO that I realized my heart was made of stone. Not only was I unable to feel anything, but I also couldn't even *think* much of anything, either. I was unable to tune in to the right frequency to continue moving forward in life.

Everything on the outside looked great. Beautiful wife, adorable kids, great big house, everyone was healthy, I had a cool little software startup in mind; it was picture-perfect.

On the inside, however, I wasn't living at all. I was only existing. I knew deep down that something was dramatically wrong. I now know that I believed this lie:

I didn't matter.

The thing is, I didn't know that's what I thought at the time, because I was so buried beneath a pile of rubble from a lifetime of battles and an ancient, unaddressed wound.

The damage I took is real and personal and intimate, the result of which almost killed me. The details of my story are mine, but the damage we all take is universal. Each one of us is damaged deep down, and that reality is what lets the lie of imposter syndrome get inside of us in the first place.

I couldn't think my way out of things anymore. I had been given a big brain and I knew how to use it, but I couldn't think my way out of this one because the place where I do my deepest thinking, the place we all do our deepest thinking, was unavailable to me.

My heart was a stone. No feeling, no thinking, no joy, no true life.

Imposter Syndrome is an imposition first on you, and then on those around you. It is imposing itself on you by forcing you into secrecy. It is growing in power because the tape in your head is playing on a loop, whispering, "You suck, you don't matter, you don't have what it takes, you have a lot of nerve even considering this!"

Ask yourself this question: *Is this true? What's the evidence I have to know it's true?*

Here's the thing: you have to be able to spot the lie in order to kill the lie.

I started to understand that my relentless focus on skillset was part of the problem. It was a singular focus for me at work, and I had a tremendous skillset and ability to expand it. But I was operating as if my skillset could get itself dressed in the morning, put its boots on, and drive itself into work. I was building tiny compartments in my life, and it was fracturing me into a distortion of what I actually am: a human being, being human.

I didn't understand that skillsets change over time, as well—what HR still calls "soft and hard skills" are what need to grow as you grow. Power skills like curiosity, compassion, understanding, conflict management, listening—there's nothing soft about those things, they are difficult! They are impossible without first understanding the importance of heartset. You can't build only hard skills—let's call them technical skills for clarity's sake—and you can't only lean on power skills. You need both!

More relentless than even my elevation of skillset, though, was my pursuit of *mindset*. Mindset matters, but it's not everything and certainly not the most important thing. For years, I drilled into my life a pursuit of growth mindset. (The ironic thing is that growth is my natural mindset and I was already doing it anyway.)

Have you ever heard anyone admit to a fixed mindset? Of course not. So stop thinking that you're actually thinking about mindset. You aren't; you're relying only on a feeling. Feelings matter, so don't ignore them; but you need to add some facts to your feelings in order to smooth them out to understand what's actually happening.

Skillset and mindset matter, but they are incomplete guides without first being powered by your heartset. The world of work wants you to be your skillset, powered by a good mindset.

At work, there is zero talk of heartset. But heartset is what makes you human. It's your deepest thinking, your deepest feeling, where language can't quite capture what you know to be true—and yet, heartset is your deepest mode of knowing what is true.

It's time to find yours, and please know, you cannot find it alone.

Compartments are isolation, and we are not designed for life in isolation. We are built for togetherness.

THE MISSION OF TOGETHERNESS

I once attended an event created by an amazing company called World50, at which the main speaker for the day was Archbishop Desmond Tutu. I found myself in a room with no more than fifty other executives all buzzing with excitement to listen to Tutu speak. It was a bucket list moment, no doubt, and one of those delightful circumstances that make me think, "If I don't learn something in the next thirty minutes, it's my fault and no one else's."

Tutu, to no one's surprise, was a delight. I came away from his talk with one concept in my head: *togetherness*.

His word for togetherness is Ubuntu. In his home country of South Africa, this word Ubuntu is important, he told us; it's the word that brought his country back from apartheid. He told us the story of how he and his dear friend Nelson Mandela handled life in their country when apartheid reigned. What held them together was the idea of Ubuntu, the idea of togetherness, the idea that we are not meant go alone in this world but we are meant for relationship with other human beings. It was his relationship with Mandela, their togetherness, that helped them survive and turn the tide of oppression in their country. None of the words I write here will do justice to what he actually said my simple intent here is to tell you about the magnitude of the moment.

At the end of his talk, Archbishop Tutu's tone became urgent and he turned his focus to the executives in the room. The executives in the room all were CEOs of global companies doing $2B of revenue per year or more. Brands like Footlocker, Subway, and Staples were present.

Tutu told us:

"If you try to go alone in this world, you will fail because it's not how God designed us. He designed us to be in relationship with Him and with each other. This is the way it works, it's the only way it works, and if you try to go alone you are trying to be less than human—you are being sub-human, in fact."

If you try to go alone, you are sub-human.

The meaning in Tutu's mission was underpinned by the power of Ubuntu; that's what mattered most. His stories were incredible and the details and outcomes magnificent, heartbreaking and spirit-lifting. It was togetherness that held it all together.

Togetherness was the meaning in his mission.

You can't be together with anyone else until you are aware and working on your ability to be a whole human being: heartset, mindset, skillsets intact and working in relationship with people you trust on meaningful missions.

You can't go alone, Tutu has it right here, and understanding the path forward is only possible in relationships.

These relationships help you know your symptoms of success, and that's where we are going in the next section of the book.

What's buried in your blind spot matters, and being held prisoner as an imposter is the first thing first. But once you're aware of this and working on understanding very clearly that you are a human on a learning curve in life and at work, then you need a simple system that supports your success over time. Willpower alone doesn't work; that's for amateurs. You, my friend, are learning about your mission, and if it matters, you need to know your symptoms of success and how to inject them into a simple system!

CHAPTER THREE

YOUR SYMPTOMS OF SUCCESS

What's the meaning in your mission? This is the question to answer by the end of this book. You need to be free of fear even to ask this question, let alone to answer it.

If you can't answer this question, or are panicked to even be asked it, go back and read through again the reality of Imposter Syndrome. You have a blind spot, perhaps, that is buried under a pile of rubble, and you might be living in imposter prison.

Even when you break out of that prison of fear, this question of the meaning in your mission is enormous. It's a huge question, an overwhelming question, one so big that it's hard to start answering because the scale of it is hard to wrap your mind around.

Remember, mindset isn't root cause solution—it's important! But not the first thing—this is a heart issue, first—heartset feeds mindset to fuel building skillsets. That's the order!

What's the meaning in your mission? And who are you united with on it? Who is together with you in it, on it, and to the very end?

Know this: you won't get your dream done without knowing the true meaning of your mission.

It is probably buried under a pile of rubble from being used and abused your whole life, but it's there, and it's real, but it's the design of how God made you to be!

What's the meaning in your mission? It must be built on truth or it won't work. Not "your truth" or your "lived experience", but actual truth.

You are the only one to answer it, but if your answer is too inward focused, that's more likely a lie, because that's not the design of how we are made.

Unless and until each person on the team has the power to go hunt for the meaning in their own mission and attach that to the work in front of them, which then is a known building block into the bigger story being told at the company, the company won't reach its potential.

This is the conversation that is not being had in corporate America. We're busy trying to solve problems like "where we work". It's an important question, but not the *most* important question.

The better question is, "*How* are we going to work?"

This question gets answered each day, although it rarely gets spoken out loud. When you have to get something done, which usually means something concrete needs to happen, you go away into a space where you can focus and complete the work.

That might be at home, it might be in your office with the door locked—it might be in the bathroom stall, for all I know—but this is what each person does when they have to get stuff done.

This conversation about where we are working is so heated that it ignores the question: "How are we working together?"

The answer is to create a power-sharing structure that supports doing work that matters with people you trust with money being made to continue the mission forward.

SYMPTOMS ARE GREATER THAN THE SYNDROME

Here's the good news: what you think is imposter *syndrome* is in fact just a *symptom*.

You aren't a fraud. You are a human being human, learning, growing, and expanding according to the manner in which you are designed—enjoy it! You're just learning something new, the results of which are symptoms of success.

The good news of the symptoms of success is that they are evidence you are not a psychopath and can feel! The next move is to add lots of facts to add to your many feelings.

Danger alert: people try to ignore their feelings in the workplace all the time. In fact, has your manager ever said something like, "Let's take the emotion out of this."

Brace yourself when you hear that, because something awful is about to happen, like someone is about to get fired and the person doing the firing wants to turn off their emotions so they can do it—it's a lie!

Fight back against this line of thinking for two reasons:

1. It's impossible to remove feelings. You are human. Don't try to become less than human, and don't ever ask anyone to try to be less than human.

2. The person that just said that to you is also trapped in a lie. You have to recognize it to help yourself, and perhaps them!

Instead of removing or ignoring feelings, add facts to your feelings.

People only do what they believe. Their words alone won't allow you to understand what's happening; you need to witness behavior, too, which takes patience.

HEARTSET, MINDSET, SKILLSET

I want you to order your sets like this:

1. Heartset: Your deepest thinking and deepest feeling that doesn't have language yet.

2. Mindset: Fueled by the thinking and feeling in your heart, let it feed your mind and use that big brain to work it out.

3. Skillsets: Both power and technical, it is the result of the fuel provided by heartset and mindset—it's hard to build new skills, after all!

Even though it's last on the list, let's first talk about skillset because it's a term that's often misused, especially in the work of leaders.

First, I want to ban you from ever using the term "soft

skills" again.

That's what HR calls the people skills: "soft".

It's ridiculous and part of the reason that few people take HR seriously.

There is nothing soft about working with people. People are seventy percent of the cost in almost all businesses, and the most important part of the outcomes companies are driving towards. Yet so often, our businesses suffer because we can't figure out how to get people going in the right direction.

Skillsets come in two types: *power skills* and *technical skills*.

Power skills are people skills.

1. Compassion: I recognize you are suffering and I want to help you get out of it.

2. Confidence: Calmness and composure, especially under stress.

3. Communication: eighty percent of communication is

non-verbal.

4. Wisdom—experience, judgement, and discretion combined.

Technical skills are the reason you have a job and the reason you'll get promoted, because companies are built to compartmentalize everything, including the human beings that work there.

Technical skills matter and need to be grown! Log in to LinkedIn right now and look at someone's profile, and it's all technical stuff—or at least that's the focus.

Here's the journey a lot of people can't make because they don't even recognize it's happening:

Typically, people get promoted due to technical expertise. But when you lead people, especially when you start being a people leader, your technical expertise in leading people is nearly zero.

This gets ignored, though, because companies have largely abandoned people leadership training. When they do focus on it, it's fluff that HR has created, and it doesn't require anyone to actually create an outcome that helps the business thrive.

How many resumes or LinkedIn profiles have you read that include the word "wisdom"?

Zero, right?

It makes sense why this isn't highlighted as earned expertise. After all, how dare you even consider that you are wise or becoming wiser—you are a big loser, don't you remember?

Another question:

Of all the leaders that you have loved working for, how many of them were wise?

Probably not 100% of them, and I'd bet anything that now you're thinking about a terrible boss that only taught you how *not* to be.

It's bizarre, but in a weird way, we love those bosses, too, because they make you want to be better (while deep down, you recognize that you probably hate them because something they do reminds you of the very thing that you believe is true for you, too—it's the lie that you made true in you, and you are railing against it).

It's easier to mad at your idiot boss instead of considering that maybe it's an issue with you, and maybe that issue isn't actually true but instead a lie from the pit of hell.

So, what if you put *wisdom* into your skillset?

Scary business, I know.

Write it down, right now.

Do it.

"Can I get wisdom? Can I get understanding?"

That's the bar and it's what the true design of being a genuine human being looks like. It's possible and it's not ambiguous or available through mystical means. It's not an "empty your mind" thing.

HEARTSET WHISPERS MEANING TO YOU

For all of the talk I do about heartset, it's because it's the most genuine path and the path that creates the best results for people and therefore companies.

Character is a heartset posture first, but it has to fuel your mindset and give you the energy to build your skillset in this area. It takes courage because you are going to discover that your character probably isn't what you want it to be and you've avoided looking at it because you secretly think it's a fixed state indictment of who you are as a person.

Your character is the thing that shows up, and yet at work, nearly 100% of the focus is on competence in "hard skills", the term that's used today (and takes you off track, as we've discussed previously).

Character gives you the ability to improve your competence through the following questions:

1. Are you good at what you do?

2. Are you learning how to get better?

If you are a leader of people, but don't consider yourself a student, your team understands that you don't value growth.

Your behavior equals your beliefs.

It's annoying, right?

This is the nature of trust in relationships. Character and competence create trust, and trust is built each day by making micro-deposits into another person's account and having them do the same for you. Sometimes the payback will take longer, but leaders must go first and more often in order to build trust with people.

If you don't have habits and routines that help you work and live more smoothly, it's harder to trust you because you'll have a breakdown at a certain level of crazy.

Think about trust as a long-span bridge. The Golden Gate Bridge has structural integrity that people trust enough to drive their vehicles across along with lots of other people at the same time. Each driver might think, "It would be a disaster if this bridge happened to collapse right now, but I gotta get to work", and they drive across it.

Are you a leader with enough structural integrity to be that long span bridge for the team of people in your care driving their vision vehicles across your bridge?

Can they trust you to not collapse?

Or are you like a country-road wooden bridge with a sign that says *Load Limit 2000 lbs.?*

The lie you've been telling yourself wants you to say the second one is right, and that might be the truth.

Make sure there is evidence for that. **Add facts to your feelings.**

And then, enjoy understanding where you stand right now—you have a baseline to work forward from—that's a win!

We will talk in the coming chapters at length about how

to gather evidence to add facts to your feelings and put them into a simple system to help you overcome these very real, deep-seated issues of the heart.

These are heart issues at their root.

All this talk of mindset misses the deeper point that your deepest thinking is done in your heart, not in your head.

Heartset is what matters first, not mindset!

When you lead with heartset, you're inhabiting the person God made you to be—a whole human not deconstructed into tiny compartments made of lies.

The tape playing in your head isn't in your head, it's written on the tablet of your heart, where your deepest thinking is done and the place where you don't have great language just yet for the ideas that are forming.

The whispers of your heart want out because they are a part of you in the same way that breathing is a part of you.

If you think mindset is what matters most, ask yourself

this right now:

When have you known anyone to admit that they are fixed mindset instead of growth mindset?

Never, right?

I did a keynote recently to a group of 1,400 executives, CEOs and CIOS alike and I asked them this question:

"So, I understand you all want your teams to be growth minded, but how many of you, right here and now in this room, are fixed mindset people? Your culture is a reflection of your leadership, so if you are frustrated by fixed mindset in your team, is it possible that you are the one with a fixed mindset? Please give me a show of hands, who here has fixed mindset?"

I had my hand raised and I was the only one in the entire ballroom with my hand up.

I stood in silence with my hand up for ten seconds—an eternity for me and everyone in the room—and then said:

"I know ninety percent of you are lying because I serve you each day."

And everyone laughed because I was getting closer to the truth.

Discussion of mindset is all the rage at work, and it's usually at its feverish peak when you or your company are going through change, and big change.

"Let's be growth minded!" you hear, and I am all for that—you have a brain, so use the thing, of course!

But it's not root cause, because it's not where your deepest thinking and feeling is done.

Your heart is not just about feelings. This is also part of the lie of imposter syndrome. Your feelings get in the way of being great at work, that's your suspicion because that's what we've talked ourselves into, isn't it?

Let me write this to you clearly: it's a lie from the pit of hell that your feelings don't matter.

Of *course* they matter! Your feelings are a huge part of what makes you human!

Relying only on your feelings, though, is a trap—you need to add facts to your feelings and work very hard to improve your character.

Heartset feeds mindset which gives you the energy to build new skillsets, all of which help you bolster up your character, which is the composite of your beliefs, morals, principles, habits, and routines that support or destroy your life.

It's your character that is designed to grow. That's the truth.

This lie you are telling yourself is subtle and it's taken root because it's believable. Defend against this by spotting it, realize it's a symptom of success not a fixed reality of who you are as a human.

This lie has been whispering to you, not yelling. You can decide to stop wounding yourself right now, to stop the chaos, at least for the moment, and work to build from the ground up according to the truth of who God made you to be.

But you must decide.

If you are not ready, I understand—these words seem too good to be true.

If you are desperate to break free of the lie, then continue reading and you will break through because the truth overcomes lies.

The lesson I learned is that there is a frequency to frequently said things, for each one of us.

When I was a CEO, deep down, imposter syndrome had taken hold of me already. I believed I didn't have the ability to be a real CEO because I had a massive amount of insecurity about not having enough integrity or character—I had fallen for a lie and it was embedded, hiding in a blind spot. I didn't understand that character is meant to grow, it is not fixed, and that I was on a steep learning curve and didn't need to panic. I needed to pause more often and search for understanding and evaluation rather than speeding ahead to application.

Which were true statements at that point! They were true about how I worked, not about me as a human being at work.

These were all just whispers in my heart, and at this stage of my game, I was nearly solely focused on my skillset. A little bit of mindset, and zero recognition about heartset.

Heartset is the bridge you must cross if you want to demolish imposter syndrome. If you aren't ready, I get it, but don't lie to yourself—you are only delaying the pain. You want to go forward, but how?

You have to cast your vision, and your vision is the whisper in your heart; it's your dream.

It's audacious and embarrassing and overwhelming because it can't be true for you because you've turned a lie into a truth and it's embedded in you so deeply that it is your default position.

You must decide to go for it.

I can't tell you what that looks like or if it's worth it, and zero amount of words I write will make you do it.

But if you don't ever let that whisper get spoken, you'll remain trapped in the terror of this subtle lie that slips in and shames you into secrecy and isolation.

THE DEEPEST MODE OF KNOWING IS LOVE

Do you think it's possible that your deepest thinking is done in your heart? Write down right now why you love the person you love the most. Name three things immediately; just react.

If you really love this person, isn't the language inadequate? Those three things are amazing, I'm sure, and very real—but are they the whole story? Of course not, because you don't have language for what love truly is—you just know it.

Love is the deepest mode of knowing, and love is the only way to dismantle the lies you have been telling yourself.

Consider your heartset today. It's the place where your deepest thinking is done and where language doesn't yet exist (which is why we settle for saying that it's where your feelings live).

What is your heartset today?

Heartset is what goes first because it's the place where your deepest thinking is done. It's the place where the spirit of God lives and is the place where deep down, you have great language but it's where you know things to be true.

Why do I love my wife?

All the language I could possibly give would be inadequate; I just know that I do. I know that I can't imagine life without her. I love her laugh, I love her willingness to see the best in everyone, I love her stubbornness, I love her beauty, and love the mom she is to our kids.

All of that is true, but it's the deepest reason because the deepest reason is called love—it's the deepest mode of knowing and that's the thinking that's done in your heart.

"But heart is all about feelings!" you say. That's what we've made it to be, and we've also convinced ourselves that feelings are bad, haven't we?

"Let's take all the emotion out of this"—how many bosses have said this? I've said it! You better know that something terrible is about to happen when someone says this to you.

Here's why it ties to imposter syndrome:

It means to compartmentalize you—to fracture you into little pieces that don't connect and that you'll ignore so that you won't be a real human being.

It's part of the lie!

Don't ever let anyone make you try and take the emotion out of your life. First, it's impossible; emotions are part of what make you human. And more importantly, they are part of your make-up that can help make you great!

Think heartset, then mindset, then skillset. The world of work wants you to do it in reverse so that you'll do what needs to be done.

Ultimately, it doesn't work and we end up treating each other terribly.

If you only ever focus on your skillset, you are a robot.

If you only ever consider your mindset, you are working hard to regulate your emotions in your mind, only.

If you start, however, at your root—in your heart, in your center, and work your way up, it's better.

If heartset means nothing to you at this point, I get it. I do think it's worth your time, though, to ask yourself one question before dismissing this point:

Why don't you value it?

If you are tempted to dismiss your heart in the context of work because the heart is all about feelings, is that actually true?

Love is the deepest mode of knowing and it's an attitude

of action done in someone else's best interest done in such a way that the person understands it as love.

That, my friend, is heartset.

You can't fake it, not for very long anyway. If your heart is crammed away, ask yourself why?

It's not crammed away, by the way, you are just working overtime to ignore it.

That general state of anxiety you might feel? It's the imposter, the lie, bearing down on you and you are generally worried it might be true. You are nearly certain your needs aren't going to be met.

When that lasts too long, you become depressed because you've moved from wondering to certainty that nothing is going to work out.

Which then shows up as anger.

Anger is a one of our emotions and it's given to us for three reasons:

1. To protect an innocent

2. To right a wrong

3. To protect or restore your dignity

But anger must be a flash, a burst of energy so you can do what needs to be done! If you stay angry, though, that's the slippery slope that compounds into this subtle lie that slips through your defense system and sets in and starts its journey from shame to secrecy to isolation to imposter and poser and maybe, in the worst scenario, to Ponzi.

You can ignore that your heart is there, or you can start to ask yourself, "Why do I dismiss this idea of heartset first?"

In my case, it was because I didn't want anyone seeing the real me. I knew if they did, then I'd be exposed as a fraud.

Remember from the beginning of this book, here's how it escalates:

1. The Perfectionist Imposter seeks perfection so that success is never enough.

2. The Poser Imposter talks beautifully but avoids doing too much so that success is never measurable; elite avoiders, this group!

3. The Ponzi Imposter is a psychopath that preys on imposters and posers that are all complicit in building a pyramid of lies.

Remember, pyramids are just big, oversized tombs for dead rich guys.

Skillsets are crucial—if you don't have skills, you aren't relevant in the marketplace.

Mindset is mandatory, too—it's just not a root cause solution.

Heartset isn't a stand-alone solution, either—but if you ignore it, it's to your own peril.

These things must unite and work together for good.

Your deepest thinking is done in your heart, where language isn't yet fully formed. What comes from your heart feeds your mind, train your mind to focus on the things that truly matter by filling it with the truth of who you are and whose you are. Then, and only then, will you have energy to build your skillsets, both power and technical.

Sixty is the new forty, friend—so you have a long way to go. You can do this work now or ignore it, but it's coming out of you at some point, whether you like it or not.

KEY TAKEAWAYS

Write down on a sticky note the following phrase:

Does heartset matter for me?

Carry it in your pocket for twenty-four hours and consider it. Then ask yourself:

Is it true that my deepest thinking is done in my heart? If I hate this idea, is it because I'm scared of what that answer might be?

PART TWO

SYMPTOMS OF SUCCESS

"We must decide each day which type of immortals we wish to be."

C.S. Lewis

UNDERSTANDING YOUR SYMPTOMS OF SUCCESS

"What are you pretending to ignore?"

This is the question I got from a total stranger as I sipped on my coffee at 7 am in a Mercedes Sprinter Van sitting curbside in New York City in 2013.

A British guy asked me it out of the blue as he sat down next to me in the van.

I was working hard to not talk to anyone at that point, it was the beginning of a long day ahead at an event and I was barely awake and enjoying the silence.

"Oh my," I murmured back to the Brit.

"It's a horrible question, isn't it?" he said. "Somebody asked it of me last week, and it wrecked me, so I figured, why not wreck you, too?"

I was in fact pretending to ignore the fact that I had to fire someone that I cared about deeply as a person, and I knew it was because I'd made a poor hiring decision in the first place and now it was going to be painful for everyone involved. I'd been ignoring this reality for six months.

"It is a terrible question and you are not a nice person to have asked me it. Who are you, anyway?"

It turned out to be Greg McKeown, the author of Essentialism, and the main speaker of the event I was attending that day!

Greg wouldn't remember this, I'm sure, but this interaction changed the course of my leadership journey. It was pivotal!

"You know what, Greg? I am pretending to ignore something and I haven't told anyone this but I'm going to go for it right now since you asked: I need to fire someone and I don't want to do it."

Breakthrough.

In this chapter, I'm going to tell you exactly how to break through, too, and to stop pretending to ignore the goals that match your role, which will help you understand how boss like a boss so you can be accountable to your mission. There are foundational ideas in Part One of this book, and if you don't consider them first, this section will only help you a little bit. I want to help you a lotta bit, so circle back and challenge yourself to consider the ideas that I present there because if you don't know the meaning of your mission, it won't matter, and if it doesn't matter, you won't care, and if you don't care, you won't make good decisions, and if you don't make good decisions, you'll be stuck in the status quo.

Here's where we are going:

1. Vision is your vehicle to get from where you are to where you want to go.

2. Mission is your vehicle's engine, it propels your vehicle forward each day.

3. Values are your steering wheel; they help you keep your vehicle on the road!

4. Goals are your gas pedal and brakes, they propel the engine of your vehicle.

5. A scorecard is the odometer, it tells you how fast you are going

6. The fuel? That's the meaning in the mission!

7. Leadership is the long span bridge that allows people to drive their own vehicles and cargo across; long span steel bridge, not a small, wooden, rickety country-road bridge.

VISION

Vision is your vehicle to get you from here to there. Write this formula down now; you will come back to these frequently from now on.

From X to Y by Z.

Your goal is to define X, Y, and Z.

In my case of the dream to become a CEO, my X was my then-current job title: GM.

- My "X": I was the general manager of a team of twenty-eight people inside a company of 20,000.

Then, my "Y" became "CEO of a real company".

- This was hilariously ambiguous, and I love it. What does a "real company" mean? To me, it meant not just me running my own consulting practice.

- As if running my own consulting practice was easy, by the way! This was the depth of imposter syndrome for me.

- I quit my job at Fiserv while making $180,000. I sold all my company stock, which was $20,000, to fund my venture—I cared zero about the tax consequence!

- I started my consulting practice and three weeks later I laid on my bed, panicked by what I'd done. No paycheck on autopay direct deposit and no idea what I was doing.

- It turns out that being a subject matter expert and running a business are two wildly different things that I did not stop to consider.

- Three years later, though, that business did $300,000 in revenue.

And yet here, in this new dream sequence of becoming a CEO of a real business, I discounted that success I had—because deep down I knew I was a fraud.

Back to our formula: from X to Y by Z.

1. From GM to CEO...

The Z is the part we all love to leave out, isn't it?

By *when?*

If you don't plug in the Z part, you have no shot at success. You need a time period in all cases here or whatever you just wrote will remain a wish, only.

I wrote down "in twelve months or less", which is insane. I had no business writing out this goal and anyone reading it would think "oh man, that's adorable, so cute" and they would have been correct!

So here's my equation: From GM to CEO in twelve months or less.

I was thirty-seven years old, married to my wife Jessica, and our son Cashel was in diapers. I was making great money now, at a job that let me work very freely, and yet here I was, with this whisper of a dream.

How would I go from running a team of twenty-eight people working on a business line doing about $17M in revenue to becoming the CEO of a 1,700 person doing $300M in annual revenue in less than eighteen months? (Yes, I missed the Y part by six months; it happens)

The real answer is by God's grace alone (which is *not* a way to say "I have no idea").

I want to give you a framework to work inside so that you, too, can understand your symptoms of success, put them in a simple system, and get dreams done on purpose, just like I did. My details are mine, and yours are yours, and the work you must do is to think this through.

MISSION

The mission is the thing that matters most each day, and if the mission doesn't matter, nothing else will, either. It's not just the company's mission, though that must mean something too; it's the meaning that you've assigned to the work that's in front of you. Unless and until that happens, the work won't be great. Meaning must exist, or what you care about won't be clear. and if that's not clear, neither will be your decision-making process—it will be muddled and so will your results. The mission has to be injected with meaning for you or it won't fuel your progress, and it also has to be move you closer to your vision each day because your vision feels ridiculously unattainable at times.

Mission: you must make it matter or it won't work! It's

still not a guarantee of success, but without deeply caring about why you are doing what you are doing, you won't be able to work through the peaks and the valleys of worklife.

Mission is the engine in your vehicle. It provides the power to propel you forward, the fuel that turns your engine is the key to discover.

Money, sex, and power are not fuel for your mission—they might get you short-term results, but nothing ever that's truly great has been built from these sorts of ambitions.

- Those are lies from the pit of hell that have gotten you off track in the first place.

- Those things aren't bad as stand-alone things to help you measure progress on the road, but if you make them the thing you value most, you lose.

- Those things won't love you back, and no amount of money will fill in the black hole of self-worth and longing for more.

The fuel for my mission then was "more!". More was my

drug of choice. I just wanted to see if it was possible to become a CEO of a real company, because at that point, I thought for sure if I could just do that, I would be making something of my life.

See the vicious loop? It's never enough, when you build upon a lie.

So, here's where I stood in my dream sequence:

Get from GM to CEO in less than twelve months, just to see if I could do it.

That's the real story, and at that high level, that's a great place to start.

The next thing I had to consider were my values: what did I value? I loved my wife, our new baby rocked my world, I wanted to make money for us, I loved working—so many things to focus on, and by focusing on too many and too many of the wrong ones, it is easy to get lost and that's when those subtle lies start to seep into your bloodstream.

VALUES

Values are your steering wheel that keep your vision vehicle on the road and not veering off into a ditch. Throw in a horn and blinkers, and you get the picture. They help you move through traffic without getting into an accident, and are the tools you use to communicate with other vehicles on the road.

So, what do you value? What do you hold out in front of you, as if it was in your hands, to be protected and treasured? Your behavior tells you the answer.

"I value my family."

But you are at work until 8 pm every night (even though you work from home, you won't get off your mobile phone)—do you really value your family or do you know that's just what you are supposed to say?

You are the only one that is going to care about what you value and really know what you value, and your values are hiding in plain site on your calendar.

Your calendar?! Yes, it's this easy.

This data is the best indicator you have right now regarding what you value and it can help you add facts to your feelings. When you have built upon a lie and turned it into truth, data can help you see the truth.

How you spend time is the best indicator of what you value.

"That's right! Get to work at 9 and leave by 5, it's just a job!" is what you'll hear from a very passionate chorus of people on social media.

If you value work-life balance—and I do—you'll realize it is the wrong term to set your goal against.

Name the number of people you know who are successful enough to be a role model that are balanced.

I'll wait.

Balanced connotes the wrong intention. Balance means that something is going to hit the ground and break, like it would on a seesaw or a gymnast on a balance beam. One wrong move, and your butt hits the floor—and it hurts!

Harmony is better. Harmony is an integration of life and work, work and life, because you recognize you can't do it all, but you *can* do what matters most and do it joyfully.

Work-life harmony is about understanding what you value and how to invest time, talent, tools, and treasure to make it happen.

Is work-life harmony closer to what you value? You must know your own answer. If we were serious about this idea, wouldn't we reverse the terms and refer to it as "life-work balance"? Of course we would, but that sounds very "woo woo"—which is another subtly judgmental phrase we use to keep us from getting to the actual truth.

You might be tempted to "should" yourself to death right now, and you for sure you will get "shoulded" to death the minute you bring this up in a public forum.

"Go should yourself" is what you can tell everyone else

for the moment, and you can say the same thing to your imposter syndrome that is banging away in your head right now.

The list of what you value needs to be short because you don't have enough time to do everything at the same time.

During the time when I was being recruited to become CEO, I kept a little list of the things I valued and used them to double check my goal list for accuracy.

At that point in my life, my number one priority was my wife, then our son Cashel—I knew already not to lump them together as just "family", it needed to be more discreet. I thought it all started first with my wife—but ultimately, that was putting her into an improper position, too, and preventing me from being in a deep, intimate, trusting relationship with her because she's a real human being, too, deeply wonderful and flawed, too, just like the rest of us.

I also valued thinking time. When was I spending time in my big picture? I've never thought of myself as extremely smart although I now know I am plenty smart enough, but I knew, and enjoyed, thinking about what might be possible.

When we moved for the CEO job, this was my list of values:

1. My wife

2. Our kids (by now, we had two!)

3. Work

4. Thinking

5. Health

6. Sleep

7. Leisure

I had no relationship with God at that point, other than a general belief that he existed and a hope that I was doing just enough to not go to hell. Health was too far down the list and way too vague.

I said out loud many times that I didn't have time to friendships with guys in our new town (massive mistake!), so it didn't make my list (furthering the isolation of imposter syndrome)

But I had a list and it forced me to think through what was important each day, and help me start in a critical practice of assessment.

"How's it going for me?" is a great question!

And if you answer it only based on your feelings, you're in trouble because your feelings are often lying to you. Facts help your feelings tell the truth.

"How's it going for the people that I love the most?" is an even better question!

What you value is up to you, so make your list right now. Take out a sticky note and write down the five things you care about most. Do it in five minutes or less, get to your version one. It is going to change many times in the coming weeks, but get it out so it can do its job in helping you navigate.

Open your calendar right now and look back two weeks:

1. No team meetings? You don't value communicating with your team.

2. No one-on-ones? You don't value personal connection with the people in your care.

3. No workouts? You don't value your health.

4. Nothing on your calendar? You don't value your time.

CHAPTER FIVE

SUPPORT SUCCESS IN A SIMPLE SYSTEM

One of my big goals with this book is that you'll be able to see the lie and kill it, add facts to your feelings as you rebuild on truth, understand the meaning in your mission, and go crush the goals that go with your role while better understanding your gifts and your gaps.

This will only be possible if you are using a simple system to support your success to overcome all the problems of being at work on the strength of your willpower alone. The simple framework is:

Vision is your vehicle, mission is its motor, values are the steering wheel, goals are the gas pedal, and meaning is the fuel.

This approach is culling the lies so you can be who God made you to be. The idea here is to further isolate your open questions so that you know where to focus and do that by destroying the isolation of the shameful lie that's held you prisoner for so long.

You are thinking through your own vision, mission, and values—now you need to step on the gas and make sure there is fuel for your mission.

In this chapter, I want to lay out the following framework for you to answer this same question:

1. Mapping out the goals that go with your role

2. How to not do your old job while trying to do your new one

3. Inspect your job description as a place to start

4. Leverage your gifts and your gaps to do great work

5. Understand all of that in the context of your company's

design

By the end, you'll have an outline to leverage so you can discover what is needed for success each day.

That's your question, too, for this section of the book— why are you the exact right person for what you are doing now and what you want to next? If you can't answer that question, no one else is going to answer it for you.

You need goals that match your role.

Write this down right now on your sticky note:

Goals match roles

After many years of doing this, I want to skip to the insight that I now use daily in my own work and the work with my clients:

The framework for your company is the exact same framework for you.

There is no difference, so your opportunity is to build your plan while understanding your company has the exact same plan in mind (although it might not be clear to you for various reasons).

There are three concepts at play for you and your company:

1. Your job description

2. Your unique gifting

3. Your gaps

Your company has a job description and one of its primary duties is to generate a profit. No money, no mission—don't get this twisted and don't make it more than it needs to be. If your company can't make money, you don't have a job.

Do you know how your company makes money? *Specifically*, not generally.

When I talk to CEOs about this stuff, this is the language I speak:

"I can measure your employee engagement from five metrics from your balance sheet."

I don't want your employee survey or the Gallup study or any of that material first. All decisions at companies are quantitative—all of the decisions involved math because companies are made to create return on investment. You can ignore that or lean into it, like I do.

It is your company's economic model, to use a fancier term. In my industry, payments, the economic model is about getting electronic transactions to occur; it's all about "swipes" of payment products like debit cards, credit cards, and now mobile phones. That's the core model and the company I ran did more annual swipes than Home Depot and we made about $.02/transaction—it's a gorgeous model!

So before you layer in any sentiment on top of the economic model, clear all the rubbish out of the way and understand how your company makes its money.

1. If you are in an advisory business (consulting), your economic model is in making sure the smartest humans on your team get sent out to customers willing to pay

for the benefit of their brain power. Keep those smart people in the office, and you lose.

2. Social media's economic model is about getting advertisers to pay for ads that you'll click on so that they can use the data you just freely gave over to serve you more ads to buy stuff you may or may not need.

You won't build great goals for your role if you don't understand your company's goals for its role.

Goals are the glue that hold companies together. It is the common ground element that everyone at the company is interested in accomplishing. Your boss wants you to crush your goals, and you want to crush your goals, because when that happens, more often than not, good things occur:

1. Promotions

2. Salary increases

3. Cooler projects

4. More interesting work

5. More interesting people

As that occurs, what also increases is expectations. As expectations increase, so will your visibility—more people will know your name, you'll have to engage more people in your projects, you'll have less immediate subject matter expertise to rely on, and you'll find yourself more often at the beginning of new learning curves.

GOALS MATCH ROLES

Goals are just good objectives with actions listed.

1. Good

2. Objectives

3. Actions

4. Listed

Don't make it complicated; make it simple and salient and you will move forward. If you don't know how the company makes money, how can you make your own goals?

If you don't know what your own goals are, how can you make them fit into the company's goals?

If you can't do either of those things, how are you ever going to help your team succeed?

Like so many things in life and at work, it's not either or, it's yes, and. You need company goals, team goals, and individual goals and they need to fit together like Lego blocks.

In this section of the book, I want to get more granular on what goals can look like for you because in my experience in all of my work, this is the hardest part for the majority of people.

What I learned, and what I want to teach you, is to spend 100% of your time, talent, tools, and treasure on the three things that matter most.

It's a game changer and seems outrageous, and it is—because at the end of this chapter, you'll have a list of things you are NOT doing.

That's your goal in this section: to list out the things you are NOT doing so that you can focus on the things that matter most.

Here, we want to overcome all the problems associated with relying on willpower alone. I have been given a tremendous amount of willpower, and one of the compliments I get all the time is about my energy: "I love your energy!"

I love it too. It's a blessing and a curse, especially when I don't recognize that it allows me to try and do everything—or at least too many things at once.

If I had ten things to do as CEO, I divided my energy among the ten things and did most of them with average results.

Priorities are for amateurs, my friends—tradeoffs are for the true professionals.

Systems help overcome problems of willpower, which if often just what we say when we want to avoid being the genuine human being God made you to be. Willpower? No! Avoidance? Yes!

Here we will build Good Objectives with Actions Listed and then give you a rule of thumb on what ACTIONs means.

Let's get practical on GOALS and ACTIONS from here and then, to finish this section, we'll build a little model to increase your confidence by measuring your return on time invested vs. the tradeoffs you are making.

GOALs are good objectives with actions listed. Objectives are lag measures; actions are lead measures.

If you don't know the goals that match your role, you have no chance at success because you have no ability to decide what's important instead of what's only annoying. Without tradeoffs, you'll get nowhere.

GOOD

- Only you know this answer and it's better for you and your boss if you take the first crack at this.

- Look back to your functional responsibilities your unique gifting and design, the gaps you have.

- Look back at the calendar audit you did already—what are the three things you'd get fired for not doing?

- Good doesn't need to be great—good is good enough! Set your "exceed goal" as the great goal, set your "good goal" as what you are sixty percent confident you can achieve, and set your minimum target at the level that everything has to go wrong for you to miss.

- Good is about using your judgement and discretion. Make your case, write it down, and move forward.

OBJECTIVE

- The key word here is OBJECTIVE! Subjective goals are mushy and hard to measure, but objective goals are concrete and measurable.

- Be objective! Use all the tools at your disposal and don't avoid the measurement.

- I'm looking at you, posers! Here, the temptation is to avoid accountability—don't do it! Break free of the lie and press on by straining every nerve to move forward.

- Perfectionists, you aren't off the hook either! That exceed goal is so tempting, isn't it? Ugh, you have energy for it and wouldn't it be great to do? Stop it, back away from the table, and go for good. There's a ton of real work to do and you are going to be pleased by the outcome and its ability to NOT fill the hole of self-worth that's been your downfall so far.

ACTIONS

- Goals without actions are just wishes, and you need to do more than wish. You have zero chance to complete the goal you set if you don't know the steps to take that add up to the goal.

- Your goal is to lose weight. Your actions include making sure your dinner plate is fifty percent vegetables. That's the level of clarity you need to succeed.

- Actions means you are going to act and act like a pro. That's right, proactive! Get on your front foot, who else is going to do it if you don't do it? No one!

LISTED

- Keep it simple and list things out and then edit to refine it down to what matters most.

- Think newsprint when you are in list mode, and go

for an accurate assessment of what will be the critical milestones to report out to ensure progress is happening.

- o Here, the temptation will be to say things like "I'm confused; I'm don't get it."

- o Yes, you do get it and no, you aren't confused. You are avoiding making progress. By this point in the book, you have plenty of tools to help you get unlocked but if you didn't do any of the work, if you didn't do the exercises I offered, that's fine—you aren't ready.

- o But don't lie to yourself that you are confused. You are resistant, and still being held captive by something and maybe that's the lie that you think is true.

- o Go back to Chapter One and see. Otherwise, abandon this book with bias and move on with your life. Just don't keep lying to yourself.

SUMMARY AND CALL TO ACTION

To execute your goals, they need to be good objectives with actions listed. The actions must bring your goal to life and always counting them is your best path.

1. What happens if you achieve them?

2. What are you NOT doing, too?

3. How are you involved? Be clear!

4. Who is else is working with you and how?

5. Does anyone care?

Keeping it simple and in front of your face will help you stop pretending to ignore what matters most. It's that easy.

If you do this work and print these things out and keep them in a highly visible space, it will be harder for you to screw it up.

1. What are the goals that match your role?

2. What is your gifting that helps your be great in
   your role?

3. What are the gaps that you have in your game?

The company I created accomplishes this with software
and services for companies. The CEOs I get to serve pay
us a lot of money to implement their own Mission BOSS,
a business operating system for success.

I'd be glad for you to take advantage of the very same
system! Just send me an email at mike@missionboss.com.
Put in the subject line "Meaning is the Mission Offer"
and then in the body of the email, what you're loving and
hating about this book so far; I want to know! Remember
to include first and last name, email, and if you want to
get crazy, your phone number, so we can be in good touch
and journey together!

THE A.C.T.I.O.N. FRAMEWORK

This framework is printable and one to pin on your wall and in your workspace. It's your playbook for moving forward and a foundational part of the simple system to help you add facts to your feelings and do only work that matters on the goals that match your role.

I make my goal and action list for the month, that way I have to ask myself each day "what did I do today to make these things happen?"

I'm not wasting time wondering what I have to do, I did that thinking in-depth one time and then I can execute it and create room to think more broadly because I'm so relaxed!

Relying on willpower alone will only get you so far. You

can use this simple system and the frameworks to help you overcome all the obstacles in your way but you have to do the work.

A = ALWAYS ACCOUNTABLE

- Accountable is a funny corporate word. It has become code for "I'll fire you if you don't do this"

- Don't run from that, lean into, and make sure you can always count the impact you are making.

- I did X to get Y by Z.

- Count! It's a math problem in its simplest version.

- 'Always' matters—be consistent, it builds your character and increases trust, and when you do make a mistake, you aren't in a deficit because it's the exception, not the rule.

C = COMMIT TO CONSEQUENCES

- What is going to happen if your goal is realized? This element needs to link back to the GOOD OBJECTIVE part in the goal sequence above.

- Someone needs to get richer and someone needs to get dinged if anything good is going to happen inside your company. It's reality. The separation between risk and reward must be enough that it will move you off the status quo path and onto the new creation path.

- Pain motivates the risk averse which is why the subtle lie slipped inside you in the first place; recognize this and build a better balance.

- What happens to people you love the most if you don't complete this goal? Anything? If nothing good or bad happens as a result, it is worth doing? Is it integral to your overall plan? If not, then don't do it!

T = TIMING AND TRADEOFFS

- This is my favorite element because this is where you witness the most lies being told.

- Do we have time? Yes or no, because the big rocks on this wall are not moving. Board meetings, client conferences, vacations, Christmas, etc.

- There are only 480 minutes in each eight hour day, how many of those minutes are truly productive?

- You must answer the "by when" part of goal planning if you want to succeed and in doing this, you'll also be a stand out because ninety percent of people leave this one to this side.

- Your daily work life is a like a bathtub full of water: at a certain point, it's going to overflow—do you know your tub's capacity? If the water runs over the side, it's going to drip down into your ceiling and cause mold and be way more expensive than anything else you are planning to do.

- This is why you must make a tradeoff, stop talking about your priorities—those are not the lead measure! What are you NOT DOING so you can do what needs to be done?

I = I'M INVOLVED

- How are you involved in this mission plan that has goals and actions listed out?

- Are you doing it? Delegating it? Or, deleting it?

- If your team is driving this goal and action daily, how are they keeping you up to date on progress? Through email on a weekly basis? That's better than nothing but it's also creating one more clog in your system of communication.

- This is why we built our software, and this is why we teach mission management and how to be a mission boss. You need to do only the goals that match your role, which includes helping everyone else do theirs—communicating progress to goal completion is the key and so answering the "I'm involved" question is job one.

- "Is this a me issue, a you issue, or a we issue, and how are we communicating progress to each other and when we are doing that?" Don't make it harder than it needs to be.

O = OTHERS, OBVIOUSLY

- Early in your career in particular, you are an individual contributor and can mostly just keep your head down and do the work assigned to you.

- As you advance, though, there are more people to consider and this is where power skills get developed, or not.

- How are others involved in your goal?

- Are they driving it?

- Are they contributing to it?

- Are they high-level advisor to it?

- Are they only FYI to it?

- Think this through and make an invitation—it is rare to accomplish a goal worth much at all without involving other humans.

- How are others obviously involved?

N = NEWSWORTHY NOW

- Think in terms of headlines and newsprint as a way to start your thinking and to support your communication because it helps you boil down to what matters most.

- Does anyone else but you care? If not, why do you?

- If they care, what do you need to tell them?

- If it's "newsworthy", go for it! But don't make it too much of an opinion piece, turn it more into a weather report.

o   The nightly news is drama.

o   The weather report is information that helps me understand "Do I need to wear sunscreen tomorrow or bring my umbrella?"

o   The weather report is newsworthy—go for that tone instead of The Enquirer.

Here's your framework to complete:

G.O.A.L. (THE OUTCOMES YOU WANT TO CREATE)

1. Good

2. Objective with

3. Actions

4. Listed

A.C.T.I.O.N. (THE ACTIONS YOU ARE TAKING TO CREATE THE OUTCOMES YOU WANT)

1. A = always accountable

2. C = commit to consequences

3. T = timing and tradeoffs

4. I = I'm involved

5. O = others, obviously

6. N = newsworthy now

GETTING A GREAT RETURN ON TIME INVESTED (ROTI)

If there's one thing that almost all leaders and people get wrong at work, it's the issue of time—there's not enough of it, and we love to ignore that fact.

Fact: you only get to ask each person on your team for 480 minutes per day. How are they spending that time?

Fact: they are going to lunch, and because they are distractable humans, things pop up (or other humans pop into their office or onto Zoom), so what's the *actual* amount of productive work hours per day?

In this section, I want to give you insight and a tool to measure your most important investment: time. It's the second most important element to understand, evaluate, and apply in all stages of work. I want to make sure you know how to invest your time on what matters most, and in this way be *effective* in your work-life, not just *busy*.

By the end of this section, you'll know how to measure your cost and output per minute, and have a proper framework to plug into your company's models to illustrate your impact, and your team's impact, on your mission.

Ready? Let's begin.

I have yet to meet a company with a time budget process. Why is that?

Do *you* have your own time budget process? Why not?

- You get paid for eight hours of work per day, that's it.

- As a leader, that's all the hours you can legally ask for from your team.

- How are you investing your 480 minutes per day?

- How many of those minutes are actually productive?

- How many of those minutes are wasted on things that keep you busy doing things that aren't productive?

This is what I want to drill home for you in regard to capacity:

Money has a budget process but if you never see any part of it, you aren't empowered to make real decisions in how you spend your time.

This is the gap and those willing to do the work to turn their bosses from authors of everything to editors of the things that matter, can win at work.

If you don't force your boss to see clearly how you invest your eight hours per day to help drive the outcomes needed for your team's success (and therefore your boss's success), it doesn't work in the way you want it to work.

This is part of the benefit of getting clear on the goals that match your role:

No one knows what the goals are that match their roles, so why not tell them what you think?

"Who I am to do that?"

Put your imposter syndrome down for the moment and do this work, it's a huge unlock for you and your boss because it's bottom-line impact work and that kind of work is how things move forward at companies.

How do you invest your time to create more money?

There is plenty of money inside corporations, it just takes some imagination to frame the opportunity well enough to act upon it!

- How you invest your time is a lead measure of your success at work.

- Invest on work that matters to the mission and that you can do the math on, and you win more than not.

- Don't, and you won't. It's that simple and that hard.

First, it's important to understand how the CEO of your company thinks about time so that you can build your plans to support it.

The more money you create for the company creates more currency in trust for you to invest your time on better outcomes. All bosses ever, even the jerkiest and the nicest, want their life to be easier because that's the nature of human beings—so make it easier by creating models that show how you will do X to get Y by Z, and then be genuinely curious about how to get that done!

Set your target goal, locate your minimum expectation and your exceed target, state your ask to accomplish, and then go execute it!

I do this with my clients and I never start working on anything until we do this work together.

What's the outcome worth? If you root that in reality, and reality at companies is found in the balance sheet, and set clear targets with the needs you have to create it, you will move things forward dramatically.

Watch how your boss's body language changes when you go through this process.

My client Ray and I did this work.

I use five metrics from his balance sheet to project outcomes.

1. Gross revenue

2. Operating expense

3. Percent of OpEx on humans

4. Number of full-time employees

5. Hours per employee per day

I do simple math on those numbers to show him his cost per person and revenue per person down to the minute per day. There's no guesswork here, these are actual numbers from his balance sheet.

I showed him that with his team of sixty-five people, he could make $1.4M in the next twelve months by increasing productivity ten percent in his employee base.

He doesn't have to do a strategy, he doesn't have to get smarter, nothing like that—all he has to do is to kill one bad meeting each day across his company and they win. For a business that does $10M in revenue per year, a million bucks means something!

"Ray, am I talking crazy here or do you follow my logic?"

"It is crazy, but no one has presented it to me like this before—but yes, I follow you, these are our numbers. How do I get the $1.4M?"

Here is the exact point where people make the mistake with their boss—in this case (in all cases), Ray is my client and therefore my boss.

The temptation is to jump into "the how" right here—don't do it. It's not what Ray is asking or what he wants.

He wants the outcome.

"Yes! That's the exact right question, but we can't answer that yet. Here's the better question. Would you invest five percent of that $1.4M in order to capture it?"

Don't you dare say a word after this statement. Relax, and be quiet.

"Of course I would!"

He has $70,000 in his head and he's thinking, "Oh man, this dude is going to ask me for $70,000."

My pricing model is nowhere near $70K but if you can't find your way to say yes to spending $70,000 to create $1.4M, something is wrong—you didn't believe me, I didn't explain it well, whatever—we can't continue until we have clarity on the outcome to achieve in the time period we want.

I'm answering for him the unexpressed problem of not knowing how much money to invest in the time we have—this framework works in all circumstances at work.

1. I used this as a SME in the implementations department

2. I used this as a team leader in the implementations department

3. I used this as an account manage with clients

4. I used this as a GM of a business line

5. I used this as the CEO of a $420M company

6. I use this today as the founder of a software and services company carving its niche in mission management

It works, and it's what can work for you, too. I'm showing how I teach CEOs to get a good return on employees, part of which is making sure the employees know how to get a good return on time invested, too. At the company, I call it ROE, for the person in the company, I call it ROTI.

Ray's question on "so how do we get it?" is a capabilities question, and if his company was capable of capturing it in the first place, I wouldn't be there talking to him because they would have already done.

Once you have quantified the "do we have time and money?" capacity question, then you can get into capabilities:

1. Do we have the skills, both power and technical

2. The tools, and

3. The team

In Ray's case, the answer was, "No, we don't have the capabilities, but how do I get them—because we need these outcomes!"

I could then lay out for him his annual cost and what he got for it.

1. Coaching for the C suite

2. Software platform to enable mission management for each staff member

3. Video based learning modules

4. Outcomes that were measured quarterly against projections

5. All within twelve months' time

I wanted to execute against the $1.4M projection—it's the most accurate number and a juicy one to sink our collective teeth into!

There is plenty of money inside corporations, it just takes some imagination to frame the opportunity well enough to act upon it and you can execute against this by dialing in how you invest your own time on work that truly matters to the bottom line.

1. From X to Y by Z

2. The goals (job description, gifting, gaps) that match the roles for

    a. Company

    b. Team

    c. Executives

    d. Staff

3. Capacity measured (time and money)

4. Capabilities measured (skills and team)

5. In order to measure plan progress in the reporting time-period.

It's not rocket science, but it is hard work because there are human beings inside a model that is working against the nature of human beings, mostly.

Humans are designed to expand and grow.

Companies are designed to consolidate decisions to reduce risk.

I made it a practice to book fake meetings on my calendar so that certain time blocks wouldn't get booked with meetings—if the time is open on your calendar, it gets taken. This was always obvious to me and without asking anyone, I just booked meetings with myself and gave them fake titles like "Project Thundergulch", so that just in case somebody got nosy, I wouldn't get in trouble.

Early in my career, I was in a big meeting with fifteen people. I was just one of the masses. The topic of time management came up, and everyone started complaining about being in too many meetings.

I just blurted out, without even looking up, "Oh, you guys don't book fake meetings with yourself so you can get work done?"

Record-scratch moment! The room went immediately silent and all eyes turned toward me.

"What? You don't do that? How do you get anything done?" I squeaked.

I had no official power; I was just a dude in a cube, and never asked anyone because it didn't occur to me. Yet I knew deep down this was against the grain of how things happened inside this company and it all came out in this moment of my public shaming.

"Who do you think you are?" said one lady from across the table. "Why would you think it's ok to do this? Do you think you're better than everyone else?"

On and on she went, and others piled on, too.

I totally chickened out and fell silent because it was an onslaught and I thankfully recognized the beating would be less bad than anything else, while simultaneously recognizing I was correct and had zero thought of changing my behavior.

I took the insults and shrunk from the confrontation, and even affirmed their insight.

"You're right, I'm so sorry, you're totally right. I see your point, yep, it's not good teamwork and I won't do it again."

Whatever I said exactly, I don't remember, but this was a turning point for me—I knew I had insight and was doing things differently and it was working, so stick with it!

I couldn't see the isolation then, but it is so clearly obvious now—the secret's power and shaming pit us all against one another. No one in that room had the confidence to say "that's interesting, tell me about that—what's working for you there, maybe I'll try it too."

Not one! It was all vitriol, and still do this day, when I do this with people they do what you are doing right now: they look at work calendars that are back-to-back meetings with literally zero minutes in between sessions, and often double or triple booked in meetings.

Just soak in that for a minute.

It's ego—*I have to be in those meetings* (even though you won't be). That's the Perfectionist.

It's insecurity—*I can't say no to these meetings* (even though you are saying no without saying no). That's the Poser deflecting accountability.

When you think about what you value, you must make a tradeoff.

If you value fitness, what are you not doing in order to accomplish it?

If you value your husband, what will you not do so that you can be with him?

When you create your values list, it must accompany the list of things you aren't valuing, too, and then you must invest that time and your calendar is the governing tool of your time at work, and you must know how to add up the cost and benefit of your investment. It's that easy, yet no one does it.

Here's your chance, and you will crush your next performance review as a result.

Are you ready to go next level and decide to get dreams done on purpose?

In the next chapter, we are going to take this work one step forward and add in your growth plan—this is where your resume meets your bucket list.

This will help you create leverage based on what you have already done in order to move toward what you want to do in the future.

Ready? Let's go.

PART THREE

GET DREAMS DONE ON PURPOSE

"THE ONLY THING TO DECIDE IS HOW TO SPEND THE TIME
WE'VE BEEN GIVEN."

GANDALF, *THE LORD OF THE RINGS*

CHAPTER SEVEN

RESUME, MEET BUCKET LIST

I worked for a manager who blocked me at every turn. She had her job for many years and she was good at it—just good, not great, not terrible.

She managed a group of implementers building databases to support ATM processing and it was pretty much assembly line work for seventy percent of the effort. The fun part was working with the clients in the process, and certainly on the day the ATM went live and processed a withdrawal, it was a great thrill early in my career.

I was in Joanne's division for eighteen months and worked directly for her for eight of those months. I'd been promoted three times already before I landed in Joanne's world, and it was a massive struggle to break free of her—which I did.

I drove her crazy and she drove me crazy. The process in Joanne's group included a multi-hundred page checklist packet to use with clients to make sure all the steps were followed—a wonderful idea! The problem? Our clients had no clue, either, and the whole process bogged down on unimportant details. After three or four projects, I understood this and just recommended the changes to the client and they usually agreed, and appreciated it.

It wasn't long before my implementation packet was more like fifty pages. I didn't ask anybody—I'm big on forgiveness instead of permission—but my primary measure of success was client satisfaction and doing my project on-time and error free.

It was easy work!

I don't remember how Joanne figured out that I'd chopped so much of the work out, but when she did, she was out for blood.

"Who do you think you are, changing all this stuff without telling me?"

I'll save you the gore because it's a total bore, but I knew instantly that I was a threat to this woman. Not once did she say "What do our clients think? What's working here better? Can we roll this out more broadly?"

Zero curious questions, and mandates to sit down and shut up and do what I tell you. Then, I wasn't mature enough to see the total picture, but I knew I needed to get away.

The insight I had was this:

How can I make the work I'm doing now overlap to the work I want to do next and not have Joanne trip me up? (By the way, no one at work is going to admit or tell you this.)

My best case for Joanne was to keep her neutral and ignoring me would be a win.

The worst case for Joanne would be for her to recognize that I wanted out and have her actively fighting against me.

Do you see the sickness here? Joanne didn't like my approach, but her results were better with me doing my job. I annoyed her, threatened her, and all the rest, but it was better than nothing because she didn't want to have to work any harder; sick!

I recognized that I was the only one that truly cared about this and was excited by it—it just seemed like the obvious thing to me: I was the only one that could make this happen.

I was a nobody in the middle of a giant organization, very early in my career with some nice early results and now making between $50 and $60K per year.

This is the reality of life inside corporate America and this is what I want to teach you in this section: how to deal in reality even with a terrible boss.

In the pyramid org chart, the top twenty percent of staff make the most money and get the most support. The other eighty percent of the pyramid are largely ignored and leaders can't "see" the talent on staff and really amazing talent comes in and goes out, all the while hidden from the people that care about that sort of thing the most!

I want to help you chart your escape path, too, and we'll do it by teaching you how to understand how to connect what you've done up until now (your resume) to what you want to do in the future (your bucket list).

FROM GOAL PLAN TO GROWTH PLAN

You are the only one that cares about your growth.

So if you want to grow, you must make your plan to grow *while* crushing your day job!

A growth plan is the plan about you and your career, and a goal plan is about you and your current job.

Growth plan: how do I move from implementation coordinator to account manager?

Goal plan: how do I implement 100 widgets this year with fewer than five percent defects?

The best bosses want to know about your growth plans and will actively talk with you about your future—embrace these humans, they are rare! Great companies have incentives tied to movement of the workforce, in particular promotions.

If your company has a formal mentoring problem, your growth plan can be more public.

If your company has formal succession planning, you are in luck; your growth plan will more activated!

More likely to be apparent on this front, however, is apathy. Sadly, your boss might work against you as you consider your career path. This is for two reasons:

If you want your boss's job, you might be a threat.

If you want a different job, you might be taking time away from the job you currently do.

If your boss is arrogant or insecure, they might have imposter syndrome and you can anonymously buy them this book and pray for a breakthrough for them. Otherwise, expect zero help from them and put all of your energy into it anyway—your boss's boss will love it.

When you consider your growth plan for what you want to next, it has to start very big and broadly, both in scope and time period—if it's too small, you won't be energized to make it happen. Way too big and it's ridiculous.

The sweet spot is to craft a vision of your growth plan that makes you say "Huh, I have a lot of nerve even writing this down, but what would need to happen for this to become true?"

It needs to make you sit up straighter in your seat, to pull you forward to make you work more deeply and smarter than you otherwise might, and in that way help you stand out among your peers and therefore be visible to the decision makers in the organization.

Of course, it doesn't always work, and there are lots of roadblocks in your way—but you won't be worse for the wear because you are building your heartset, mindset, and skillsets to be relevant in many more areas of life and work, which helps you get into better conversations about what problems need to get solved next.

What are you doing today that is like this? This is outside your normal goal plan and dead-center of your growth plan—they complement each other, and your goal is to make them cross-over more each day.

The trick, though, is to not make them get out of balance, especially if you are working at a company. Companies hire employees to create output. Don't get this twisted and don't misunderstand—this is a good thing, especially now that you can do the math!

Put these pieces I've been discussing with you together and you are starting to see the shape of your mission plan. Your goal plan is mostly about your work and your growth plan is mostly about your life—put them together and you have a clearer view of your work-life.

- Not just feelings, but facts.

- Not just activities, but outcomes.

- Not just functional responsibilities, but your unique gifting and your gaps.

- Not just problems, but challenges with activities that creates results on time.

- Not just goals, but activities that bring them to life.

There will be moments in your future that you can't anticipate now, but all this work will prepare you to meet them when they appear.

That's the work you have to do in your growth plans—this work is the pinnacle importance in your work-life journey but it's a mistake to make it the primary thing—that makes it out of order.

Crush your goal plan and your growth plan is easier.

Work on your growth plan first and more than justified, and it's obvious you aren't doing the first thing first and so will never realize the promise of what might be.

SHOPPING CARTS

Goal plans are for your daily work, growth plans are your career. You need both, and at first they might not connect to each other. That's ok. Your goal is to integrate what you do daily to what you want to do next. This section helps you create your path to success.

You don't want to do the same job, but the hiring manager wants to know you've already done the job they need done. Your work now is to help your audience (the hiring manager, your boss, whomever) to understand how to connect the dots from your work history to your work future to increase their confidence that you can do it.

In this section, you are going to build your CART stories and use your CARTs as your compass. What's hiding in plain sight is that you've already done things in your past that can help you in your future; the trick is to see the themes that connect you from where you are to where you want to go.

This is a huge opportunity, but you'll miss it if you don't

do the work to identify what you don't know. This whole process is designed for you to call out and systematize what you know and must do so that you can handle all the variables that surprise you each day with greater effectiveness.

The challenges every person has at work can be batched up into big themes, and these big themes are what you'll hook your CART stories to in order to help people see why where you have been is helping you get to where you want to go.

Every hiring manager ever wants the person they hire to already have proven experience in solving the problem they have right now—it's human nature. That manager is in pain and they want a painkiller to make it stop.

If you have already seen and solved that problem, you are an attractive candidate for that hiring manager.

But if there are no new problems for you to solve, only the old problems, there's nothing new for you to learn and with nothing new, it will be boring and ultimately, spirit crushing.

With CART stories, though, you will help yourself connect the dots from your resume (what you have done) to your bucket list (your dream job).

CARTs help you get there.

Problems that impact the balance sheet are the ones that get worked on at companies, so if you can't tie the challenge you are facing to the results you need to create, you are wasting your time.

In this section, you'll learn a simple equation that will help you do that.

CEOs think in outcomes, not activities, so you have to tell your CART stories in that format, first, and then be prepared to support the details as questions arise.

If you were a newspaper, think headlines first, then newsprint. If your headline is clickbait, you lose.

This is your format: Challenge, Action, Result, Time

Period.[1]

1. Challenge: what problem are you solving? Be specific.

2. Action: what actions are you taking to solve the challenge? Think "restaurant menu" and not chef's ingredients list. What's coming out of your kitchen and onto the table for dinner? That's the thing to discuss!

3. Result: what do you think is going to happen? Or what did happen? Root it in reality and if you can't add up the growth or the savings, don't waste your breath, it's not getting approved. Zero big decisions at work get made without a business case.

4. Time Period: by when? A goal without a deadline is just a wish.

It's not just CEOs to consider. In the biggest picture, all companies and hiring managers have the same kind of challenges and your goal is to connect the challeng-

---

1   I've based this on a tried and true problem-solving technique called CAR that is most commonly used to perfect one's resume or hiring interviewing skills.

es you've seen and solved in order to increase the hiring manager's confidence that you can do what needs to be done while not boxing yourself in to just doing your old job again (even if for more money).

CARTs are your compass. They create continuity and confidence. They add facts to your feelings. In big, thematic ways, what you have already done gives evidence that you can do what needs to be done next. But, if you never write them down and put them in story form, you are trapped in the muddle of your feelings, only.

Our CFO was great at CART stories. Here's one of his classics:

"Mike, I've been studying our financial operations and it costs us 3.8 percent of operating expense to run it. Our peers operate at 2.3 percent and so I see the difference as a lack of process and automation over the last few years. I'd like to reduce our expense by one percent over the next six months and need $175,000 in order to do it. I'm hiring a process expert consultant and know we'll need to upgrade at least two of our systems and figure we can shed at least three to five others. Can I proceed on that?"

That's how you present a CART story! Done like that, it helps you have great conversation because it's in a format everyone can follow.

As you work on the exercise below and build out your list of CART stories, you'll start to see themes emerge regarding the big challenges you've solved in your career so far. That's good!

Here's your big question to make this all worth it:

Which of the challenges that are part of the next job you want have you already conquered?

READER PRACTICE

To do this well, I want you use five things:

1. Your phone timer, set for sixty minutes

2. A pen

3. A legal pad of paper

4. Your big brain

5. The deepest thinking in your heart

In sixty minutes' time, you'll have a list of the challenges you have identified, the actions you took to solve them, the results those actions created in the time period measured. Then, we will work to help you use these CART stories in helping you navigate your way forward.

Read this next paragraph and then set your timer for a sixty minute countdown. Then get to work and don't stop until the timer goes off.

On your legal pad, spend your first fifteen writing down all the challenges you've seen in the last one to three years. List them down the left side of the paper. Don't worry about judging them or measuring them or anything else. Just jam on it and get a list of problems you have faced on the page in front of you.

Then, in your next twenty minutes, go back through that list and write down next to the challenge (aka the problem!) you faced and then list in three to five words the action you took to solve the problem.

Your imposter syndrome will rage here! Ignore it, you champion, and be willing to toot your own horn—if you don't, there will be no music!

In your actions list, don't write the words "we" or "us" or anything like that—I want you to write down what *you*, dear reader, did to solve that challenge.

In your final twenty minutes, go back through your list and add in a results column next to the challenges and actions you took. Results are what matter at work, so show your work here.

Lastly, write in the time period you are measuring. This bit is the part that was missing in the original idea I read so long ago, and it is a *huge* gap in nearly everyone's thinking at work, especially those suffering with imposter syndrome.

"By when?" If you don't state the time period, it remains a wish. If you've made it through five chapters by now, you know to be more rigorous than that!

Ok, here's where you take your courage in both your hands, set your phone timer for sixty minutes (put in in airplane mode), and get to work. It should be an ugly, organic mess of ideas and results and problems solved and timing; we'll clean it up later.

UNLOCK THE WISDOM AT REST INSIDE YOUR COMPANY

In 2013, I had an amazing opportunity to meet Hank Haney, the number one golf coach in the world at the time (according to people that know golf, anyway), and he just finished up a run coaching Tiger Woods, the number one golfer at the time, too. Hank had just published a book and our company hired him for our client conference outing. It was a day of golf at Torrey Pines in California for our clients, each one of whom got to meet Hank and get a mini golf lesson.

The deal was for Hank to be at one of the Par three holes

for the whole round of golf, and for 120 of our clients and their spouses to come through and meet him and get the mini lesson.

It was fascinating to spend six hours watching this all play out, and it led to a fifteen-minute micro-mentorship by Hank to me as we rode on the golf cart back to the clubhouse. I barely talked to Hank during the six hours at the hole, but I was going to take advantage of the time we had on the drive back. I wasn't supposed to be on the cart with him, but just said "Hank, might if I grab a ride with you back to the clubhouse?"

Here's what I witnessed watching Hank work with our clients:

He had an elite ability to make people relax in his presence—this was his gifting. His job description was golf coach, and his gift was to make people relax so they could be taught

It was incredible and very obvious from the first person until the last. Hank was a golf celebrity; he had had a TV show, was Tiger Woods's coach, and published a book. If you liked golf, you knew exactly who this dude was. Based on the 120 reactions I watched, our golfing clients were overwhelmed to meet him.

All these CEOs and powerful people, and they were knee-knocking nervous to meet Hank Haney and have to swing a golf club in front of him! I loved it and could have watched this for another twelve hours because Hank was masterful at this one thing, first:

He made everyone relax.

He'd give each person one great "swing thought" (a term Hank would later explain to me) and then encourage them to give it a go.

I was deep into my ability to be clear on the goals for my role as CEO and worked hard to identify what tradeoffs I was making, and in this way had isolated the open questions that remained to be answered over time.

One of my open questions coming into that day was, "How might I overcome the problems that come with the stereotype of CEO in order to understand what's actually happening in our business?"

When any boss walks into the room, the mood changes because the boss ultimately impacts your career path and paycheck—everyone is on their best behavior, in other words. Which limits the ability to see things for what they are instead of what you want them to be.

I knew by then that because I was CEO, I was instantly smarter, more handsome, fitter, and funnier than was actually true—there's a fakeness to it that is alluring and yet also a trap.

So, I was very interested in understanding that dynamic and not shrinking from the responsibility of being CEO, and instead how to optimize it.

I had been working up to this point on understanding with greater effectiveness simple things like avoiding the wrong meetings—I needed to stop trying to be everywhere at once and more involved in work that only my role could accomplish.

When I went into meetings, then, how might I contribute to the outcomes we needed and help to move things forward?

All of that and more was on my mind, and then *boom*, there I was witnessing this experiment in humanity. I knew instantly this was a target rich environment:

I was going to say hello and thank you to 120 people that were our clients.

It was a gorgeous day in California and all I had to do was stand there and enjoy it.

My role that day was to not be in the way, but to be a support—the star of the show was the golf and the teacher, Hank Haney.

I realized immediately Hank's ability to make people relax—this was generally the same open question I had on my list of things to get good at for my role.

There was almost no way I was getting on the cart with Hank for the ride back.

I thanked him, of course, and we had two minutes of chit-chat, and then I went for it.

"Hank, mind if I ask you a question about today?"

"You bet."

"Ok, here's what I saw: it seemed to that three types of people came through today—one group basically ran up to the tee box, swung the at the ball, and ran away—they couldn't get it over fast enough. There's another group that seemed very interested to blame you for everything bad that happened, which, by the way, I want to apologize for because some of them were kind of rude. And then there was a small group—I only counted three people all day—that shut up long enough for the possibility that they might learn something from you and it seemed to me, that they also looked like the best players. I know almost nothing about golf, but that's what I saw—am I crazy to make those observations?"

To my surprise, he laughed!

"Ha! Oh man, Mike, that is great—I've never thought

about it like that! First of all, that was some bad golf, some really bad golf—but I think your point is interesting. Say more."

At this point, there's enough common ground, and plenty of time left for my one big question, so I asked:

"Okay, but here's the thing that I was so impressed with and want to hear you talk about if you can, please. Your ability to put everyone at ease immediately was incredible! Obviously you are a great teacher and very clearly a celebrity to golfers, which I didn't appreciate until I saw how people were reacting to you, but I was blown away by your ability to break through all that in sixty seconds or less and help people relax. Is that intentional? How do you do it? Can you talk to me about that?"

"Huh, that's so interesting—usually people want to talk to me about golf. You sure you don't want to talk about golf?"

"I really don't, if that's okay—I want to learn how you do that, it's a gift and I want to know if it's natural or developed?"

I could see Hank's body language relax now, and he started talking. I barely said a word for the rest of the ride. He told me how he's learned to disarm people, from an expert like Tiger Woods to be a beginner like one of our clients that day.

"I just tell people, 'Look, you aren't going to impress me with anything you do and you aren't going to embarrass yourself by being terrible because I've seen it all, so let's just take that off the table right now.'"

He understood how to kill imposter syndrome right then and there! Take away the fear, and good things can start to happen.

Take away the fear, and you can recognize that an elite teacher is right in front of you. You can recognize that it's time to stop talking and start listening, because he might have the crucial wisdom you need!

There is wisdom at rest inside your company. If you understand how to unlock it for your benefit, you can get nuggets of knowledge from which to chart your course. If you know how, you can turn anyone into a mini-mentor, even the jerks, and do this on a daily basis to build new power and technical skills to flex throughout your career and in this way, create the antidote to imposter syndrome.

More than simply skills, development, though, this path is a profound way to understand and deepen your heart and mind sets—there are no compartments, there are only humans being and with this concept, you are able to practice being human.

By the end of this chapter, you will have a framework to help you engage nearly anyone at your company to work on three things at once:

1. Your goal plan (the daily work that adds up to the company's mission)

2. Your growth plan (the work you want to do next)

3. Making goal and growth plans unite by increasing your understanding of the big picture and your ability to evaluate where you are right now—and then making anyone a micro-mentor to help you test the sturdiness of your thesis

IMPOSTERS STAY ISOLATED

Why haven't you already done this? What's in your way?

1. It might still be the lie you think is true.

2. It might be that you don't know what goals go with your role.

3. It might be that you get lost in the day-to day whirlwind and let your to do list dominate your life.

There's lots of reasons, and most of them have solutions laid out in the book, but it's up to you to do the work.

Do the work, and it will happen.

Don't do the work, and continue to suffer.

It's that straightforward.

Your job is not to pose as someone else; your job is to be

who God made you to be.

1. Be who God made you to be.

2. Do the goals that match your role.

3. Use a simple system that supports your success.

That's the overarching theme of this book and in this micro-mentorship question, you are leveraging the wisdom at rest inside your network, and more importantly, inside your company, to test and learn the sturdiness of your thesis.

What's working, what's not, what's next?

What better way than to go talk to other human beings who have already been where you want to do to seek understanding of what might also work for you?

Here are two reasons this strategy won't work for you:

1. If you think it's weakness to ask other people what they know, what you think you know will then prevent you

from learning something new, and

2. If you don't know generally the open questions in your mind and be willing to ask them out loud, you won't be able to connect any dots because the people you talk to won't have any targets to shoot at specifically.

Remember: imposters are isolated, and they stay that way by not asking for help. Reject that lie, and open yourself to the wisdom at rest in your company. We're built to learn, expand, and grow. Don't make this harder than it needs to be.

THE MICRO-MENTOR METHOD

In my experience, one of the keys to great micro-mentorships is the span of time in your career blocks—too much distance (fifteen years apart of career tenure), and it's hard to recognize each other. Too close, and there's not enough difference in what you know to make much of a difference in your work-life today.

The sweet spot, very unscientifically, seems to be seven

to ten years. That person is just a little bit ahead of you in their journey (or you are to them), and so you can ask them questions that will resonate because it's not so far in their rearview that they'll be guessing and that you'll understand it as relevant because not so much has changed since they did what you are wanting to do.

Going into the meet-up, I know the big questions I'm wondering about in my business. I know where I stand in my overall mission plan, I have clarity on goal progress, I have confidence and curiosity in both my gifting and my gaps.

I'm settled, in other words, and can enjoy conversation with another human being. I've been doing this for twenty-plus years and it's working; the only difference now is that I have a name for it.

Here are keys to consider:

- It's not actually about the person sitting across from you, primarily—it's about your ability to connect with them in manner that they understand and relax into so that you can ask them open-ended questions that they'll want to answer.

- Resist the temptation, however, to find an answer in this one meeting. The answer you are looking for is hard to find or you would have found it already—this is one twenty-minute meeting, with one person.

- In this model of micro-mentorship, the payoff for you comes when you meet with seven different people of all different backgrounds and then can assess all the feedback and look for general themes to consider for you.

It's like talking to Yelp Reviewers in person instead of reading their feedback online. When choosing a restaurant for the best hamburger, it's not worth it to spend 140 minutes talking with seven different people about the burger (although I do love a good burger!)

So why do it here? Well, this is your life and your career and if you don't want to spend this little bit of time getting smarter about how to make good decisions, then this might be why you are in the boat of confusion in the first place.

From this perspective, why would you NOT do this?

Another key to this model is to embrace the fact that not every meeting is going to result in gold—you'll have some clunkers and feel like you wasted the twenty minutes. Don't worry about that, it's why it's only twenty minutes—it's practice!

This pattern is the one for you to follow.

1. You know what you do

2. You need to get a quick outline of what this person does

3. You need to see the common ground and identify what's different

Get good at this and it takes five minutes or less.

Now your goal in the next fifteen minutes is to validate your high-level thesis and to direct the conversation generally toward the open questions in your business.

The power-skill to develop in micro-mentorship is to have a format that helps you move through these conversations with enough consistency to allow you to be curious in the conversation. No format, and it's all ad hoc; you won't make progress, and it will exhaust you.

As with so many ideas, I am pretty sure I've taken then best twenty minute meeting format from *The 20-Minute Networking Meeting* by Marcia Ballinger and Nathan Perez. I recommend this book to everyone looking for a job. They have an amazing script on how to do the twenty-minute meeting, including their concepts behind how to make twenty minutes with another human matter most.

They want to help you get another job. I want to help you get smarter about the things you are not yet smart about.

I've turned this into my own twenty-minute meeting and I plan for micro-mentorships in this way:

1. First two minutes: welcome and hellos, thank you, then set the table for how we want to spend our time together.

2. Next fifteen minutes: open-ended questions on interesting nuggets from the opening responses.

3. Final three minutes: recap, take-aways, follow-ups

You will be surprised at how much ground you can cover in the meaty part of the fifteen minutes. You won't be able to do that, though, if you don't prepare, set the frame for success, or ask open-ended questions and then shut your mouth to listen to what the other person says.

It will just be another fifteen minutes of you talking.

Of your imposter talking for you.

Don't do that. Be confident, be concise, be curious, look for things that connect to your world that this person has more expertise in than you and then go for it.

This is the perfect setup for micro-mentorship.

We are spending twenty minutes to figure out if it's worth spending another 90 minutes together.

We had a mutual "a-ha!" moment, and could now understand that it was worth pursuing.

My goal in this book is to help you use a simple system that helps support your success, part of which is helping you free up time and energy to find the answers to your remaining questions.

Up until now, you have been spending too much time getting tangled up on the obvious things like "what goals go with my role?" If you are wandering around on that front for too long, you are wasting time and now you know why: you have been pretending to ignore the lie that became true for you.

Now, in micro-mentorship, you can bring that out into the open even more and finally extinguish it. You will be tempted to be on your social media blaring your new found insight to the world—don't do that.

Instead, do the harder thing, which is to sit with human beings and talk to them about these open questions in your world and ask them how they've tackled the same kinds of challenges, and then be genuinely curious about what they tell you!

Ask your question and stop talking, friend! Listen. Be

curious. Be interested. Don't be embarrassed or ashamed, be a student!

You don't have to sit down and tell anyone, "Listen, it turns out I'm a big fat loser that thinks he's a total fraud because I don't know how to be an elite leader."

Re-read that sentence out loud for yourself.

It's silly, you are hearing it correctly.

First, you need someone to admit that to, no doubt. But it is intimate, personal, and to be shared in trust with someone in your inner circle.

Maybe there are three such people in your life, but if there are more, you are lying again to yourself.

READER REFLECTION

Identify five people at your company that you perceive are great at doing one-on-ones. Ask around, collect a list of people, and make them your targets for twenty-minute meetings.

1. Who runs great meetings?

2. Who seems calm and capable?

3. Who, without saying any words to you, do you admire?

In other words, who do you have a workstyle crush on?

You are going to meet with all of these people over the next six weeks. You are going to use a consistent approach with each one of them and ask them the very same question and you are going to spend fifteen minutes of each meeting listening to how they solved the problem you are studying for yourself. Do not admit the deep-down struggle here yet—it's none of their business and will only be a distraction. Most people will want to spend their time talking you out of the lie but will be "normalizing" it instead for you. This is the way it goes at work and it's the reason I don't want you to post this on social media. It's fake feedback that does not help you grow.

What helps you grow is understanding and evaluating your relationships with other human beings.

Here's your approach:

1. Name your role models: shoot for five and not more than seven names.

2. Name your question, but do not overly personalize it and make it about you; that will take you off course.

3. Name one reason to connect with each person and make it good enough so they'll say yes to a twenty-minute meeting.

4. More than twenty minutes at work and most people recognize thirty minutes means forty-five minutes, and most people don't have or want to spend that much time on anything not directly related to their world.

5. Twenty minutes, though, is novel and most people, with a clear agenda, will say yes.

6. Name the one question you want answered and ask it open-endedly in order to get your person talking more

broadly about how they do things.

7. Resist the temptation to talk. Too much talking by
    you means not enough learning for you.

You can do this model with all of your outstanding items
in your journey with me so far.

1. Wondering what goals go with your role? Ask someone
    that you admire on this front "it seems to be from afar
    that you crush all your goals, am I crazy in thinking
    that? How do you do it?" Who doesn't want to answer
    that question?

2. Wondering how to lead people that are older than
    you? Ask your role models "I don't get to be up close
    and personal in your world very much, but it seems like
    you've made fast progress in leadership journey. What's
    worked for you as you think about leading teams of
    people that are much older than you?"

You have fifteen minutes, it's not enough time. Ask a good
question and actively listen to what the person tells you.

What they tell you might not apply to you. What they tell you might be dead center interesting to you. You must ask them in order to know either one. Don't chicken out; you have what it takes!

DECIDE TO GET DREAMS DONE ON PURPOSE

By this point in our work together, you can see the lie. You dismantled it. You are building on truth, finally.

Now your work is to turn these little moments into momentum by injecting meaning into your mission.

What's the meaning in your mission? I'm hoping by now that question is in your heart and working its way up to your mind and soon, out of your mouth and into your actions because it's the whole ballgame. Know the meaning in your mission and you can't be stopped, you won't be stopped.

This is the open question for you to answer and I hope what makes this whole book worth reading for you. This question takes a long time to answer, and the answer will deepen and change and there will be many plot twists, but unless you know this, the rest of it doesn't make sense.

Work as we know it is a paradox:

- Humans are made by design to learn, expand, and grow— you can most easily see that in our children.

- Company work is made to be the opposite—to constrict decisions to reduce errors to reduce expenses to increase profitability.

A dream without a plan remains a wish, but a dream with a plan turns into your mission.

Once you have your mission, you are motivated, and once motivated, you won't be stopped.

Here are the questions you are working to answer. Keep these in front of you, get them into your bloodstream, and you will grow, learn, and expand—because that's how God designs his humans!

1. What does all of this mean to you? Why does it matter? What is the meaning of your mission?

    a. If it's going to work and become inevitable, it must mean something to you!

    b. How do you connect your own, personal meaning to the work you are assigned and connect it to the company's meaning? This is how to unlock massive value!

2. What are your symptoms of success?

    a. What's going well? What's not?

    b. How do you know? Add facts to your feelings!

3. How would anyone else know what success is?

    a. What is your definition of success?

    b. Is it clear or ambiguous? Ambiguity is your

enemy!

   c. Is it shared by others?

4. How do you do more of what's working for you?

   a. Surface and solve the problems standing in the way of your shared definition of success.

   b. Too many surprises = no system, ad-hoc approach, and weak leadership and management skills.

5. How are you ordering your focus?

   a. Heartset is where you deepest thinking is done

   b. Mindset is fueled and made more concrete by your heartset

   c. Skillsets are built from there, both power and technical

d. Keep this order and don't go in reverse, and certainly don't fall for the lie that your heart doesn't matter or that it's only feelings.

6. Are you clear on your Vision, Mission, and Values? Do they mean something to you or not? No meaning, they won't get done!

   a. Vision is your vehicle to get you from here to there, and

   b. Mission is its motor; can you rev the engine? And,

   c. Values are the horn, airbags, steering wheel, and brakes.

   d. Can you drive it on the open road?

7. Do you know the goals that go with your role?

   a. Your company's goals are in Vision, Mission, and Values.

b. You have functional job responsibilities.

c. You also have unique gifting and gaps.

d. Make these things converge more each day!

e. Good Objectives with Actions Listed: Listen while always being accountable, committing to consequences, understanding timing and tradeoffs, knowing how you are involved with others, obviously, and nailing the newsworthy now and you are in business as a top ten percent performer in your company.

8. Are you doing your role in rhythm with your company?

a. Thinking "Lego building blocks", your goals and role must 'snap' together as a building block in your company.

b. Your year has a rhythm, it's not a sprint—map it out so you can dance together!

9. What is your plan to connect your Resume to your Bucket List? This is your Growth Plan!

   a. Your daily focus goal plan synced to your career growth plan helps you navigate toward work that makes each thing move forward, and you are the only one capable of doing this and the only one whose interest it is in—enjoy this work!

10. How are you unlocking the wisdom at rest inside your network to find the answers to your open questions? Who are your micro-mentors and what is your simple system to gain the benefit of people that are smarter than you on a given topic? Build this muscle and you can't be stopped!

11. How are you packing all of this into Mission Management?

   a. The mission has to matter or it won't get done.

Dream your vision, put a plan around it to turn it into your mission, assign the goals and actions that make it come true.

You have symptoms of success, not a syndrome of fraud. You might feel like a fraud, but that's because every great lie is subtle enough to slip past your sniff test because there's enough truth in it—you might not know what you are doing, this is called "learning something new!"

This subtle lie sets in and starts to shame you because it's very clear to you that you are the only freak with this problem.

The shame makes you keep it a secret so that you'll stay isolated, and the more you stay isolated, the better chance for the lie to become true for you. Once it becomes true, you have a blind spot—you can't see the problem anymore because it's not a problem, it's true for you.

It's not a syndrome, though, and when you work to add facts to your feelings, you start to understand these are feelings that generally happen when you are the bottom of a new learning curve.

A lie needs an absence of infrastructure to grow. It needs

you to do things like saying "let's remove all the emotion out of this" so that you'll drift toward being subhuman.

It needs you to believe that your skillset is that matters, that your skillset can get itself dressed and drive into work—more drifting towards compartmentalizing you, chopping you up into smaller and smaller pieces, like you are an album on iTunes with individual songs for purchase.

Lies need you to believe based only on your emotion and that emotion is buried deep down in places that you don't want to discuss so that you'll overreact to it and destroy yourself slowly and then quickly.

It needs you to believe that anything you do isn't good enough, perfection itself included, because you aren't worth a shit and you know it.

It needs you to believe that you can never own your outcomes, good or bad, because judgement is coming and that report card criticism will be an indictment of who you are, which very clearly is a poser.

To set in, the grand lies need an absence of truth and the world is working hard to make sure your soil is barren.

Instead, you must understand that you have symptoms of success and your simple goal is to understand them to make them more systematic to support your life and work.

A simple system to support your success and help you overcome the problems of working on the power of willpower alone by dreaming your vision and injecting it into your mission management system.

Here is the simple system that supports your success in your work-life journey:

1. Imposter syndrome: the lie you believe is true for you.

   a. Perfectionist, poser, or Ponzi—this lie must die.

2. Symptoms of success: add facts to your feelings to understand the greater truth.

a. Get out of isolation and into student mode: you aren't a fraud; you are just learning something new!

3. Heartset first so it can feed your mindset which fuels your energy to build new skillsets!

    a. Your heart is where your deepest thinking is done, where language is not all the way formed yet—listen to it, and let it feed your mind with truth and not lies! Train your mind then and harness both to help you assess your skills, both power and technical, and build from there!

    b. Do not do this in reverse, skills aren't the first thing and if you never admit you might be fixed mindset, you are continuing to lie to yourself. Break free of this!

4. With these building blocks in place, where you do want to go and what is your vehicle to get there? Cast your vision, that is your vehicle!

a. Put a plan around your vision to make it your mission because your mission is your vehicle's engine, you need to step on the gas!

b. Values help you keep your vision on the road and not veer into a ditch, while the meaning of your mission is the missing link:

c. Meaning is the fuel of your mission—without it, it won't work.

5. Goals match roles! Know yours!

a. Don't do your old job, do your new one!

b. Snap these together like Lego building blocks with your teammates and watch how much easier it is to work together.

6. In this complex world, a compass beats a map, so make you CART stories be your compass.

a. Challenges: faced and conquered, understand them!

b. Actions: what did you do in the face of the challenge?

c. Results: what impact did you make? Add it up, it's what you and your company need—it's the currency of progress at work!

d. Time period: by when, for goodness' sake? A dream without a plan remains a wish, and a plan without a deadline doesn't get done.

7. A simple system supports your success, and helps you overcome the problems associated with relying on willpower, only.

   a. GOALS + ACTIONS: Good Objectives with Actions Listed, rooted in always counting the outcomes with consequences understanding how everyone is involved in what time period on what matters most.

8. Your resume must meet your bucket list in a growth plan you build and tailor to your career growth. You are the only one who can do this, so

don't wait.

    a. Help yourself by helping your company, first.

    b. Make your CARTs converge with your Goal Plans, and then make your Goal plans over-laps to your Growth Plans more every year.

    c. You don't have to announce it, just do it!

9   Make anyone a micro-mentor in order to unlock the wisdom at rest inside your company. You have worked hard to make more things known, now you have time to dig into your open questions—what better way that to ask another human being who has already been where you want to go?

    a. Ask the same question to seven different hu-mans and look for the themes to test in your work-life. Measure them, see what's working, abandon what doesn't and double down on what does!

10. Transform from Imposter to I'm Possible!

a. Meaning is the fuel to your mission, know it to make it inevitable.

b. You see the lie and know to kill it, you learned a simple system to support your success and are on your way to becoming who God made you to be because now, you are building on truth!

The greatest confidence signal is that you become coachable, that you grow from feedback, because you now can understand and evaluate better who you are, where you are, where you want to go and how to make progress toward it.

At this point, though, you don't need more facts, do you? You need to go and do, so go and do. Take your courage in both your hands, you have things from this book that are proven to work—but no one is going to do it for you.

This is your time. It is right now.

What's going to be different if you want to be different?

CONCLUSION

I began this book by asking three big questions and offered you three modes to know if I'm telling you the truth. I hope by now you have at least some answers to the questions and a path to find the ones that remain open for you.

We are the end of the book, but you stand at the beginning of what's next for you.

This book is about you in the context of your company and is focused on providing understanding and evaluation instead of blind application in the hope of advancement. I want you to easily achieve a 3x to 5x return on your time invested here (and you now have an equation to answer that for you—it's your ROTI!)

Companies are spending more money than ever on employee engagement and it's getting worse because we are solving symptoms and not root cause. Now you know the root cause and can own the path to solve it—don't wait on anyone, this is your time!

"Is *the way you work* working?"

- You are not an imposter; free yourself from that prison of fear.

- Break that blind spot wide open and build on truth, not lies!

You have symptoms of success and an ability now to add facts to your feelings and understand that your behaviors equal your beliefs.

"Are you working on what matters most?"

- Unless and until you make your mission matter, it won't work to the level of your dreams.

- Meaning is the fuel for your mission. Inject it into your plan to make it go!

- Vision is your vehicle, mission is its motor, meaning is the fuel and goals are the gas pedal.

- Success is a simple system, build yours to support your success so you'll overcome all the problems associated with relying on willpower alone.

Do the goals that match your roles, only!

"Are you also working on what's next?"

Now you know the path to go next level while working on what matters today—do it!

- Unlock the wisdom at rest inside your company and sync your resume to your bucket list!

You know how to make anyone a mini-mentor now so isolate your open questions, find your role models, and meet with them to consider this evidence that you can add to your mission plan.

Your last step, but your everyday first step, is to then decide to get your dreams done on purpose. You busted out of prison, you have three modes to know and one mode of go, and you have a simple system to support your success. You are getting into your vision vehicle and revving your mission's engine. Put the fuel of meaning into it and step on the goals-that-match-roles gas pedal, and get on with it—get to the work now and stay on until the very end!

I am cheering for you, I am praying for you, and I am so thankful that you read my book! I hope it helps you get your dreams done on purpose!

AFTERWORD

Writing this book was the most fun, creative thing I've ever done, and it was also the hardest. I'm excited to write the next two books that go with this one!

None of it would be possible if I didn't do my number one job each day, which is to let God love me completely and intimately, involved with everything and anything, nothing too big or too small, so I can be his message. I am known, and I am loved, and I am here because it's what God wants and is what gives him delight, and so who am I to shrink from my place in line? Do I have to stand on the street corner with a bullhorn and I sign saying that? No. So why say it here?

I'm saying it here because it's the truth that makes this whole book make sense, and that's because it's what makes sense out of life.

This is God's good creation and I am in it because of him, that's it and that's all. I get so fired up to read Genesis 2:19 and know that we are made namers! God is collaborating with his people, and his creation works when we are obedient in doing our number one job each day. Then, and only then, can we love one another with even a hint of how much God loves us.

My prayer for you is that you come to know him more deeply each day because you realize that you are first known by him, created by him, put here in this time and this place for his purpose and reason and that you are built to be in a relationship with him so you can be in relationship with his people, too. You are not built to go through life alone; that's what Tutu's tough love was all about.

I am excited for you and what is happening in your life, and I can't wait to hear how the ideas in this book challenged, changed, or confirmed your thinking. I would love to hear from you whenever you are ready.

I am grateful to God for the ability to write this book, and in that way, start a relationship with you. Let God love you today, and each day, so you can be his message in his Kingdom on earth as in Heaven!

ACKNOWLEDGMENTS

I am grateful to God for him and his good creation, that I am known and loved by him! Those words are true and my heartset and also prove the point that sometimes, words can't express fully what you know to be true!

Without my wife Jessica, this book and all the good things that go with it would not happen—this is a woman I love, I know, I trust, I believe, and I am inspired by and her support throughout this process has been amazing— each night on our walk together, she would say "it's gonna be great!" and I would believe it even when I didn't believe it. Fav, you are my Fav, thank you for marrying me!

Our kids, our "Team Kid", inspires me each day and is one of the great joys of being alive! Cashel, Maebyn, and Colm—I love you, I love being your Dad, and I love participating in helping you become who God is making you to be!

To all the people I've worked with over the years, the good bosses and the bad, getting hired, fired, and promoted, it's all been amazing, and each moment is amazing even when it was terrible.

To my trusted and Dangerous friend Dave Ruth, the man who told me the gospel truth and helped to save my life, I love you my brother and I am grateful to God for you! Your unwavering support, encouragement, critique, and insights are all things that words can't truly capture but I know are love in its purest form. I am with you, too, through to the end!

To my dear friend Tim Keiningham, who from the first minute I met him, always shoots me straight and is unwavering in his belief in me—like the rest of this list, I don't have words but only love.

To my mom, Mary Kelly, who got it done for her family against all odds, and helped to get me to where I am today by showing what love looks like even when the words are buried under Irish Catholic rubble, your strength of character will last for many generations!

And to you, the reader of this book—I hope I get to meet you one day and hear about how you got your dream done on purpose.

ABOUT THE AUTHOR

Mike Kelly is the founder and CEO of TeamOnUP, the company bringing Mission BOSS into the world of work. TOU is a software and services companies with a mission to unite people on purpose, and is working to always be the bar setter in the Mission Management industry.

Mike and his wife Jessica, along with their three children Cashel, Maebyn, and Colm, make their home in Franklin, TN. Mike was born in Pittsburgh, grew up in New Jersey, graduated from Florida State University, but is certainly from Tennessee.

Mike is also a sought-after keynote speaker and is looking for to going global with the message of "Meaning is the Mission".